# INNOVATION & INTEGRITY

## THE STORY OF

# HUB GROUP

# INNOVATION & INTEGRITY
## THE STORY OF
# HUB GROUP

**JEFFREY L. RODENGEN**

Edited by Ann Gossy
Design and layout by Ryan Milewicz

Write Stuff Enterprises, Inc.
1001 South Andrews Avenue
Fort Lauderdale, FL 33316
**1-800-900-Book** (1-800-900-2665)
(954) 462-6657
www.writestuffbooks.com

The publisher has made every effort to identify and locate the source of the photographs
included in the edition of *Innovation & Integrity: The Story of Hub Group.* Grateful acknowl-
edgement is made to those who have kindly granted permission for the use of their mate-
rials in this edition. If there are instances where proper credit was not given, the publisher
will gladly make any necessary corrections in subsequent printings.

**Publisher's Cataloging in Publication Data**
*(Prepared by The Donohue Group, Inc.)*

Rodengen, Jeffrey L.
   Innovation & integrity : the story of Hub Group /
Jeffrey L. Rodengen ; edited by Ann Gossy ;
design and layout by Ryan Milewicz.

     p. : ill. ; cm.

   Includes index.
   ISBN-13: 978-1-932022-24-7
   ISBN-10: 1-932022-24-4

1. Hub Group (Firm)—History. 2.
Containerization—History. 3. Freight and
freightage—History. I. Gossy, Ann. II. Milewicz,
Ryan. III. Title. IV. Title: Innovation and
integrity V. Title: Hub Group

TA1215 .R63 2007
385/.72/065/0973        2007923526

Completely produced in the
United States of America

10 9 8 7 6 5 4 3 2 1

# Also by Jeffrey L. Rodengen

The Legend of Chris-Craft

IRON FIST:
The Lives of Carl Kiekhaefer

Evinrude-Johnson and
The Legend of OMC

Serving the Silent Service:
The Legend of Electric Boat

The Legend of Dr Pepper/Seven-Up

The Legend of Honeywell

The Legend of Briggs & Stratton

The Legend of Ingersoll-Rand

The Legend of Stanley:
150 Years of The Stanley Works

The MicroAge Way

The Legend of Halliburton

The Legend of York International

The Legend of Nucor Corporation

The Legend of Goodyear:
The First 100 Years

The Legend of AMP

The Legend of Cessna

The Legend of VF Corporation

The Spirit of AMD

The Legend of Rowan

New Horizons:
The Story of Ashland Inc.

The History of American Standard

The Legend of Mercury Marine

The Legend of Federal-Mogul

Against the Odds:
Inter-Tel—The First 30 Years

The Legend of Pfizer

State of the Heart: The Practical Guide to
Your Heart and Heart Surgery
with Larry W. Stephenson, M.D.

The Legend of Worthington Industries

The Legend of IBP

The Legend of Trinity Industries, Inc.

The Legend of
Cornelius Vanderbilt Whitney

The Legend of Amdahl

The Legend of Litton Industries

The Legend of Gulfstream

The Legend of Bertram
with David A. Patten

The Legend of Ritchie Bros. Auctioneers

The Legend of ALLTEL
with David A. Patten

The Yes, you can of Invacare Corporation
with Anthony L. Wall

The Ship in the Balloon:
The Story of Boston Scientific and the
Development of Less-Invasive Medicine

The Legend of Day & Zimmermann

The Legend of Noble Drilling

Fifty Years of Innovation: Kulicke & Soffa

Biomet—From Warsaw to the World
with Richard F. Hubbard

NRA: An American Legend

The Heritage and Values of RPM, Inc.

The Marmon Group: The First Fifty Years

The Legend of Grainger

The Legend of The Titan Corporation
with Richard F. Hubbard

The Legend of Discount Tire Co.
with Richard F. Hubbard

The Legend of Polaris
with Richard F. Hubbard

The Legend of La-Z-Boy
with Richard F. Hubbard

The Legend of McCarthy
with Richard F. Hubbard

Intervoice: Twenty Years of Innovation
with Richard F. Hubbard

Jefferson-Pilot Financial:
A Century of Excellence
with Richard F. Hubbard

The Legend of HCA

The Legend of Werner Enterprises
with Richard F. Hubbard

The History of J. F. Shea Co.
with Richard F. Hubbard

True to Our Vision
with Richard F. Hubbard

The Legend of Albert Trostel & Sons
with Richard F. Hubbard

The Legend of Sovereign Bancorp
with Richard F. Hubbard

Innovation is the Best Medicine:
The extraordinary story of Datascope
with Richard F. Hubbard

The Legend of Guardian Industries

The Legend of
Universal Forest Products

Changing the World: Polytechnic
University—The First 150 Years

Nothing is Impossible: The Legend
of Joe Hardy and 84 Lumber

In it for the Long Haul:
The Story of CRST

The Story of Parsons Corporation

Cerner: From Vision to Value

New Horizons:
The Story of Federated Investors

Office Depot: Taking Care of Business—
The First 20 Years

The Legend of General Parts:
Proudly Serving a World in Motion

Bard: Power of the Past,
Force of the Future

# TABLE OF CONTENTS

# FOREWORD

BY

## MATTHEW K. ROSE

CHAIRMAN, PRESIDENT, AND CHIEF EXECUTIVE OFFICER
BNSF RAILWAY COMPANY

AS ONE OF NORTH AMERICA'S largest railroads, the BNSF Railway Company transports more than five million intermodal shipments on its 32,000 miles of rail routes each year. BNSF moves more intermodal traffic than any other rail system in the world. We load a container onto a BNSF intermodal train every six seconds of every minute, every day, and we trust Hub Group to fulfill a significant portion of our intermodal needs.

When the railroads first deregulated in 1980, Phillip Yeager, founder of Hub Group, proved instrumental in pioneering a model for how the railroads should work with intermodal customers. His ability to collaborate with the railroads and his unparalleled integrity served as the model for all third-party intermodal marketing companies (IMCs). Phil has seen the industry through the worst of times and the best of times, and his stellar leadership has guided Hub Group through the necessary changes that are reflected in the company's successful business model today.

Beyond that, Phil is the type of person you can trust with a handshake deal. When he gives his word and says he is going to do something, you can take that to the bank.

Shortly after the Burlington Northern and Santa Fe Railways merged in 1995, the leadership team at BNSF recognized that intermodal offered a great growth opportunity for us. We decided to explore different types of intermodal partners. We considered working with businesses that had their own assets and those that didn't. After the railroads deregulated, there were literally hundreds of third-party intermodal marketing companies in existence. We thought strategically about which businesses would succeed long-term in the third-party channel and which ones had the potential to become industry leaders.

We decided to align ourselves with Hub because the company had evolved from a decentralized, entrepreneurial, family-owned business into a publicly traded, centralized organization that could successfully handle both scale and consistency.

Hub had also experienced an information technology transformation that involved a $50 million investment, which enabled it to aggregate its business and utilize our own network. Although industry analysts were uncertain the large investment would pay off, it did. Hub made a big bet on technology, and without that large gamble, Hub would have been just another among the hundreds of third-party providers in the industry.

I believe the most significant event for Hub involved the company's decision to become the first IMC to test, evaluate, and then implement an asset-based model. Both Phil and David Yeager were willing to take the risk and invest first in leasing and then in purchasing containers when no one else in the business was willing to do it. As a result, BNSF's relationship with Hub has grown from our first order of 3,400 containers to the 12,000 containers Hub now manages exclusively for BNSF. This business arrangement has allowed us to take our market share with Hub from around 32 percent in 1988 to about 60 percent in 2006.

On this 35th anniversary of Hub Group, I congratulate Hub Group and its leadership team on their strong commitment to the railroads, their excellent customer service, and their willingness to take risks in the highly competitive intermodal market.

# ACKNOWLEDGMENTS

**M**ANY DEDICATED PEOple assisted in the research, preparation, and publication of *Innovation & Integrity: The Story of Hub Group.*

Research Assistant Richard Knight conducted the principal archival research for the book, while Senior Editor Ann Gossy managed the editorial content. Graphic Designer Ryan Milewicz brought the story to life.

Several key individuals associated with Hub Group provided their assistance in development of the book from its outline to its finished product, including: Phillip Yeager, David Yeager, Mark Yeager, and Thomas Hardin. Maralee Volchko served as our tireless and efficient liaison. A special thank you goes to Matthew K. Rose, chairman, president, and CEO of BNSF Railway Company for contributing the book's foreword.

All of the people interviewed—Hub Group employees, retirees, family, and friends—were generous with their time and insights. Those who shared their memories and thoughts include: Brian Avery, George Baima, Lillian Barrone, John Bauer, David Beasley, Mike Blackwell, Steve Branscum, Mike Bruns, Mike Carrol, Joni Casey, Jim Comerford, Stephen Cosgrove, Jim Decker, Donna Dick, Stanley Dick, John Donnell, Joe Egertson, James Gaw, Jim Gibson, Thomas Hardin, Dan Hardman, Ron Hazlett, Tom Holzmann, Harry Inda, Dennis James, Debra Jensen, Robert Jensen, Jim Klingberg, Christopher Kravas, Jim Lee, Thomas Malloy, Donald Maltby, Jr., Donald Maltby, Sr., David Marsh, Mike McClellan, Chris Merrill, Dick Merrill, George Olson, Ed Peterson, Terri Pizzuto, Dennis Polsen, Steve Rand, Tom Reisinger, Dick Rogan, Jim Ronchetto, William Schmidt, Connie Sheffield, Jude Troppoli, Joe Wallace, Thomas White, George Woodward, Anne Yeager, David Yeager, Mark Yeager, Phillip Yeager, and David Zeilstra.

Finally, special thanks are extended to the staff at Write Stuff Enterprises, Inc.: Stanimira Stefanova, executive editor; Elizabeth Fernandez and Heather Lewin, senior editors; Sandy Cruz, vice president/creative director; Elijah Meyer, graphic designer; Rachelle Donley and Dennis Shockley, former art directors; Roy Adelman, on-press supervisor; Lisa Andruscavage, proofreader; Mary Aaron, transcriptionist; Elliot Linzer, indexer; Amy Major, executive assistant to Jeffrey L. Rodengen; Marianne Roberts, executive vice president, publisher, and chief financial officer; Steven Stahl, director of marketing; and Sherry Pawlirzyn-Hasso, bookkeeper.

Uncle Sam pulled Phil Yeager out of college in 1946 and drafted him into the Army. Phil never saw combat since the war ended before he was ordered to go overseas.

# CHAPTER ONE

# BIRTH OF A BUSINESS DYNASTY

## 1927–1970

*She said, "Where should we go?" and I said, "Chicago. It's the only place. It's the hub."*

—Phillip Yeager

PHILLIP YEAGER HAD NO IDEA that the company he would create with his wife, Joyce, would become an industry giant. Yet, since its founding, Hub Group has become the largest intermodal marketing company (IMC) in the United States and one of the largest truck brokers. Through the company's network of dozens of operating centers, Hub Group has the ability to move freight in and out of every major city in the United States, Canada, and Mexico. Strategically, from its beginning to the present, the company has remained "asset-light" even as it serves many of the Fortune 500 companies.[1]

All this was far in the future when, in 1971, Phil found himself at a career crossroads after 19 years of working for the Pennsylvania Railroad. He spent most of his rail career serving as an assistant director of piggyback transportation (a term that would eventually morph into intermodal).[2]

But for Phil, a secure job at the railroad did not provide him with sufficient personal satisfaction or great financial rewards. "The railroad was not big with the salaries," he remembered about his financial position at the time. "To be honest, we were personally going into bankruptcy. I had to do something." Despite the additional expense of sending his eldest child to college, and less than one year left until Phil could collect his long-awaited pension, he seriously contemplated leaving the

security of his full-time job to pursue his dream. Phil felt that his career with the railroad had come to a standstill, and he decided it was time to make a decision.[3]

Phil's early biography reveals a history of risk taking and a frustration with a perennial "second-best" status in both his work and athletic accomplishments. Phil explained:

*I was always the number-two man, and I'm a very competitive person. It seemed like it was a pattern in my life. I thought starting my own company was something I could be first at.[4]*

His career with the railroad paralleled the rise of the intermodal industry, in which he had become expert. The early intermodal industry, too, held second-class status in the transportation field. Competitive in the extreme, its shipper agents were often described as pirates and cutthroats. "Neither the railroad nor the shipper agents trusted one another," Phil said.[5]

Nevertheless, he sensed in this perception of second best a sizable opportunity. He suspected that an intermodal business built on strin-

Phil Yeager's high school yearbook photo from 1945.

gent ethics and loyalty, the values he and his wife, Joyce, shared, was bound for success. Decades later, Phil attributed his resolution to venture out and succeed to the unfailing support and urging of his wife: "Joyce was my inspiration for work. She had complete confidence in me, which gave me confidence in myself."[6]

So, in 1971, Phil and his wife and children moved from New Jersey to suburban Chicago, the "hub" of the intermodal transport business. The Yeagers had $500 in their pockets. Phil was 43, the age at which most successful businessmen start planning their retirement.[7] Instead, he and his family embarked on an entrepreneurial journey of a lifetime.

### Back to 1927: An Industry Leader Is Born

The tiny hamlet of Bellevue, Kentucky, just one-mile square, is located on the bank of the mighty Ohio River directly across from Cincinnati. The town, a suburb of Cincinnati, was settled by General James Taylor, a Revolutionary War hero, and named after his farm, which stretched from Bellevue to nearby Newport. Taylor's mansion is still a favorite stop for historical enthusiasts. The General also took responsibility for naming most of the town's streets, including Fairfield Avenue, the town's commercial thoroughfare.[8]

By the end of the Civil War, much of the Ohio River Valley (including Bellevue) became home to a large German immigrant population.[9] On November 15, 1927, Ferd Yeager, a gregarious former car mechanic turned butcher, and his wife, Helen (Koehler), proudly announced the birth of their son Phillip. A daughter, Beverly, had been born two years before, and another daughter, Jean, would follow two years later. Phil was the only son of the young, hardworking couple who toiled side by side in their butcher shop.[10]

Phil's grandparents had immigrated separately to the area from Germany when they were in their early teens. They settled in Bellevue on Center Street and opened a butcher shop, which occupied the front portion of their home. After Phil's parents married, they took over the butcher shop. Though Helen only had an eighth-grade education (as did Ferd), everyone in the family concurred that she was the brightest of the children—

A wedding portrait of Phil Yeager's parents. Ferd and his wife, Helen (Koehler), married in 1923 and settled in Bellevue, Kentucky.

brighter even than Phil's three uncles who had all become doctors. "My uncles always told me that my mother was the smartest one in the whole family," Phil recalled. "She was the caretaker of her brothers and sister."[11]

Phil remembered his childhood in Bellevue: "As a kid, you didn't dare get into trouble because everyone would know. Everybody knew everyone else's business. The whole town was like a huge family."

These were the years of the Great Depression when money, especially in a working-class town like Bellevue, was tight. By the time he was nine, Phil recalled helping out in his parents' butcher shop by delivering meat each day after school and on weekends:

*For a delivery, sometimes I'd get a nickel or a doughnut. No one had any money, and I was happy to get what I could. Everyone called me the "Butcher Boy of Bellevue."*[12]

Phil had a talent for sports, and he played football, basketball, and tennis throughout his high school years. His athletic skills earned him a scholarship to the University of Cincinnati in 1945.[13]

### An Unfortunate Accident

Although Phil attended the University of Cincinnati on a joint football and basketball scholarship, he soon discovered he wasn't big enough for football, being six feet three inches but only weighing 175 pounds. During his fourth game, Phil, an end, played a few minutes on the third string at an away game against the University of Detroit. Following the uneventful game, Phil and several of his fellow teammates headed up to Windsor, Ontario, at the nearby Canadian border for a bit of ice skating with some enthusiastic female fans.[14]

Phil had never ice skated before, but that didn't stop him from heading out onto the ice to impress one of the girls in the group. "Out of the blue, a young boy about nine or 10 came flying by," Phil recalled. "He flipped me up in the air, and I came right down on my spine." He added, "Talk about pain. Wow, that was horrible! I've had a lot of injuries in my lifetime but nothing like that."

The incident occurred five days before his 18th birthday. Phil broke two bones in his spine, experiencing pain for a long time as a result of the injury, which slowly healed over the next 10 years. Phil's athletic ambitions had come to a sudden end.[15]

### Uncle Sam Comes Calling

Early in 1946, Phil found himself drafted into the Army. "Even though I was in school, they drafted me," Phil said. "All the vets wanted to get home, so they were bringing us kids in. As long as you could walk through the door, they took you."

The Army sent Phil two-and-a-half hours south of his home for tank training at Fort Knox,

Kentucky, and later transferred him to Fort Lawton in Washington. He had learned how to drive the M-26 tank. "Not well, but I could drive it. That was relatively new then," Phil recalled. "It wasn't as good as the German tank, but it was still a fine tank. I was lucky to miss out on the original tanks they fought with in Europe. They were just a piece of tin when they went into combat against those Panzer divisions. But the M-26 was very effective."

Phil and his fellow soldiers prepped for action and waited for orders to head overseas to fight against the Russians, who had invaded the Aleutian Islands. But President Truman and Russian Premier Stalin resolved their differences diplomatically, and instead of combat action, Phil received his discharge papers 18 months after being drafted. He returned to school, but this time decided to focus on studying economics.[16]

### The Girl in the Pink Dress

Back at the University of Cincinnati in late 1947, Phil kept up with his studies and played on the tennis team, though he no longer participated in football and basketball due to his ice-skating mishap. At the time, Tony Trabert captained the tennis team, and he went on to win the United States, French, and Australian Open. "Everybody on our team was a state champion in high school," Phil remembered. "And I was very happy I was a part of it."

But something much more memorable occurred one evening when Phil sat on the street corner while passing the time in Bellevue. He recollected what happened: "A young lady I had been dating was walking up the street with three other gals. So I met up with her, and we were talking, but she didn't introduce me to this one young lady in a pink dress

During a break from military training, Phil Yeager traveled to Colorado Springs and visited the famous Broadmoor Hotel.

on the side. I thought she was such a cute gal and very talkative."

Phil escorted his girlfriend home, but couldn't resist asking her about "the girl in the pink dress." The girlfriend claimed she didn't know her, but Phil persisted. Again, she maintained ignorance of the mystery girl's identity. Phil continued, "I kept quizzing her, and as I got up to her door, I said, 'Can I come in?' and she said, 'No,' and 'Whack!' right in the face. Never dated me again."

Undeterred, Phil persisted in his search and soon found out his mystery girl was Joyce Ruebusch. He asked her out on a date, and that first night, they walked into an ice cream parlor for cones. Phil remembered:

*We went in and I said, "Let's get the big cone," and she said, "No, I just want the little one." I bought her a 10-cent ice cream cone. I really knew I had met my future wife.*

Later, when Joyce said she preferred walking the few miles home to Dayton rather than taking the bus, it confirmed for Phil that he'd found his perfect match: a confident beauty who knew what she wanted and wasn't afraid to go the extra mile to get it.[17]

Phil experienced two important events in 1951. First, he graduated that spring from the University of Cincinnati with a bachelor's degree in economics. Then, after a year-long engagement, he married Joyce Ruebusch on June 2, at her hometown church in Dayton, Kentucky.

Above: A charming couple, Joyce and Phil were married on June 2, 1951. They are pictured here at their reception in Dayton, Kentucky.

Right: While living in Fort Wayne, Indiana, Joyce proudly holds the Yeagers' firstborn child, David.

During this time, Phil worked as a warehouse manager with Pure Carbonic Company, producers of dry ice and carbon dioxide gas. The job lasted only during the summer, and Phil didn't "much care for it." He wanted year-round work to support his new wife. When a friend mentioned a job possibility with the Pennsylvania Railroad in 1952, Phil applied and got the job.[18] Phil had no idea his life's work was about to begin.

### A Budding Career

The railroad wasted no time in sending the Yeagers to Chicago where Phil worked first tracking cars for the railroad (thus the job title "tracking clerk"), and later as a file clerk. This was the first of nine moves Phil would make during his career with the Pennsylvania Railroad, or PRR, as it was more commonly known. Soon after this first move, the PRR sent Phil back to Cincinnati for a short stint and then had him return to Chicago. In late 1952, after an eight-month period in Chicago, the railroad sent him next to Fort Wayne, Indiana, for a two-year assignment. Then, on March 19, 1953, the Yeagers welcomed their first child, David, into the family. In 1954, the railroad uprooted Phil and his family again, this time back to Chicago. Phil, enthusiastic about the hard work and long hours, soon moved up the ladder to become assistant office manager.[19]

The year 1954 prompted a significant change for the railroad industry after a ruling by the Interstate Commerce Commission (ICC), which tightly controlled the industry, finally granted the railroads permission to transport truck trailers from point to point. Previously, railroads weren't even authorized to take an item as simple as a trailer and put it on a flatcar. This new form of shipping—called piggybacking—was a boon to the industry. Piggybacking involved transporting goods in trailers wired to flatcars that were transported by rail throughout the

# THE ABCS OF INTERMODAL

THE YEAR 1954 MARKED THE EMERgence of a new form of shipping called piggybacking. This innovative approach to transportation involved moving goods using the traditional railroad, but carrying them in a novel fashion. Instead of physically packing railcars with goods shipped to the railroad by truck, the actual truck trailers, already filled with goods, were loaded onto the railroad flatcars. The railroad then carried the filled truck trailers, wired to the flatcars, to their destination.

Piggybacking, so named because the trailers literally rode on the railcars, later developed into what is known today as the intermodal transportation industry. The term *intermodal* refers to transporting goods using more than one mode of transportation—including rail, truck, airplane, and ocean carrier—without removing or repacking the goods from their original containers.

Train cars were a great improvement on the original flatbed carriers, and the railroad industry quickly embraced them.[21]

### Growing Success and a Growing Family

In 1956, Phil earned another promotion, this time to a sales representative position. The PRR moved Phil and his family to Kansas City, Missouri, where he single-handedly covered a large territory. He received an expense account of $135 a month, but his boss insisted he spend six days on the road each month selling. "It toughened me as an individual and helped me appreciate a good job, because this was not one," Phil commented. Though Phil experienced little joy in his work, he and his wife savored happiness in 1957 with the birth of their only daughter, Debra.[22]

In time, Phil would finally have an opportunity to see the burgeoning intermodal industry up close. By 1959, his hard work paid off, and he was promoted to assistant director of sales for the PRR's nascent piggyback division at the railroad's corporate home in Philadelphia. Phil explained:

The age of intermodal was ushered in with the widespread usage of piggyback trailers like this example from the Burlington Railway.

country. Phil recalled his excitement with this new transportation concept:

*Right from the beginning, I was so excited with intermodal. In fact, I saw the very first full train that went out of Chicago. It was something that I was interested in immediately.*[20]

Along with the new form of shipping came new service divisions for the railroad. A lucky employee of PRR won a $500 prize for naming the trailer on flatcar service division TrucTrain. In 1955, another division called Trailer Train (now TTX, Inc.) introduced the first railcars specifically designed to carry trailers. Prior to this, they were strapped on with wires. The new Trailer Train cars held their trailers by stanchions, which were upright steel posts that supported the loads. Trailer

*When the railroads tried to sell their own services, they couldn't do it. The railroads had put in very attractive ramp-to-ramp rates in an effort to stimulate intermodal shipments, yet they didn't know how to sell intermodal as a concept. They tried to compete with truck lines by offering the same service, and supposedly the same rates, but people wouldn't buy it. The railroads needed another party, a shipper agent type—today we're called intermodal marketing companies—to make all of the arrangements on drayage, equipment, and everything else.*[23]

In his position with the railroad, Phil worked with shipper agents, many of them independents, who competed against each other for the opportunity to arrange intermodal shipments with the PRR. During this period, freight forwarders and truck lines were tightly regulated. The shipper agents had much more freedom. "They had no regulation, which gave them the ability to be flexible and actually sell the railroad product to shippers," Phil recalled.[24]

While in Philadelphia, in 1964, he and Joyce welcomed their second son, Mark, into the family. Phil's growing family did not distract him from continuing to hone his natural sales and networking abilities, and he experieced continued success.

After five years in the position of selling intermodal for the PRR, Phil was again promoted—this time to division sales manager—and he and the family moved to Milwaukee, where they lived for another three years.[25]

In 1968, the Pennsylvania Railroad and the New York Central Railroad experienced deep financial difficulties and decided to merge, becoming the Penn Central. This merger, a last-ditch effort to save both of the once-mighty transportation giants from receivership, would serve as a catalyst to end Phil's career with the railroad.[26]

While the merger occurred, Phil, still in Milwaukee, proved a natural salesman for intermodal shipments. He explained:

*That wasn't my only role, and I was criticized for focusing my efforts on selling intermodal shipments. I was in charge of all services, but I would always say to my boss, "You asked to get 3,000 carloads of freight, and I got 6,000 new trailers this year."*

*I dealt with shipper agents while I was with the railroad. I got to know a little about the business. I liked it. The business was very entrepreneurial and had considerable flexibility. Everybody wanted to get into intermodal.*[27]

At the time of the merger, Phil requested a move back to an online position because he felt stifled at the offline level. He experienced frustration because advancement prospects passed him by. "I thought opportunities would be zilch in an offline position," he commented. "I told them, 'If you want me, I'll go anywhere in the railroad, but I have to come online.'"

After Phil declined a move back to corporate headquarters in Pennsylvania, the railroad came up with the promise of a $45-dollar-a-month pay increase if he would move to New York. "I really had

Left: This vintage advertisement sells the benefits of TrucTrain, the PRR's first trailer on flatcar service division.

Above right: A Yeager family photo taken in 1959. Back row left to right: Phil; Joyce; Phil's mother, Helen; Phil's grandmother, Edna Koehler; and sister Beverly Moore. Front row: Daughter Debra; niece Vicki Moore; nephew Michael Moore; and son David.

no choice," Phil remembered. "I had to go. I had to do something." David, the family's eldest son would soon enter college, so money had become more important than ever. For the ninth time, Phil and his family packed their belongings and moved again, this time to Cranford, New Jersey. Phil worked in New York for the company's inter-modal division (renamed Trailvan), and again as the number-two man.[28]

### A Business Dynasty Begins

At this juncture in his career, Phil recognized that his well-honed knowledge of the shipper agent side of the railroad business placed him at a decided advantage if he decided to break out on his own. "I knew the shipper agent business inside and out," Phil said. He continued to encounter frustration as a result of his perennial second-place status and lack of financial reward:

*I was second team all-conference in football and basketball and runner-up in tennis singles in the Kentucky state championship in high school. It was time for me to be number one.*

One night, Phil came home and voiced his feelings to Joyce: "I told her the merger was absolutely ridiculous and said, 'I'm going to leave the railroad as soon as I can.' I realized there was no future for me there."[29]

Joyce knew that her husband—after 19 years of service with the railroad—was a year away from locking up a supplemental pension. But, over the years, she saw his ceaseless frustration and strong dedication to work. Without missing a beat, she responded, "I'm ready." The two discussed Phil's longtime dream of starting his own shipper agency. "I thought this was something I could be first at. I saw a real opportunity here." Phil later reflected, "I had an idea I thought would work, and I thought I knew more than any of my competitors."[30]

The couple discussed where to begin anew. Phil recalled:

*After I dismissed Joyce's ideas of moving to Miami or San Francisco, she said, "Where should we go?" and I said, "Chicago. It's the only place. It's the hub."*

So in the spring of 1971, Phil quit the rail-road, and with $500 in cash, his 19 years of on-the-job training, and Joyce's faithful support, the family struck out for Chicago, the hub of the trans-portation industry. They packed everything they owned and shipped it to their new destination ... by piggyback.[31]

Hub outgrew its tiny office above the florist and moved in 1973 to a larger space above a laundry establishment in nearby Clarendon Hills. These are recent pictures of that building.

# CHAPTER TWO

# BEGINNINGS

## 1971–1975

*All they heard at home was "Hub, Hub, Hub."*

—Phillip Yeager

HINSDALE, ILLINOIS, LIES 19 miles west of Chicago. This conservative, upper-middle-class suburb,with its tree-lined streets, expansive lawns, good schools, state-of-the-art hospital, and country club with a renowned golf course, boasts a large number of private and public buildings on the Hinsdale Historical Society's list of designated landmarks.[1]

At the north end of town stands the Graue Mill, built in 1852. Now restored to its original appearance, it serves as a statewide tourist attraction. Each year, it draws thousands of visitors who come to view the vintage reenactment of a typical day in the life of the mill. Abraham Lincoln is said to have visited the site during his presidency, while on a trip from Chicago to Springfield.[2]

From 1847 through 1861 alone, a network of 11 separate railroad lines branched out from Chicago. They spurred the creation of Hinsdale and other nearby towns that sprung up along their tracks. By 1873, more than 100 railroad suburbs surrounded the Windy City.

Purchasing 6,400 acres of land in 1862, William Robbins planned and built streets, landscaped parks, and planted shade trees along the quiet streets in anticipation of the arrival of the commuter railroads and the influx of residents to follow, eager to leave the noise and crime of the city behind. The village Robbins planned, then called Fullersburg,

fulfilled his vision of creating an American version of an English country village. Today, Hinsdale's colonial-inspired town hall and library still provide a gateway to the village's picturesque downtown area, and looks much as it did when Phillip Yeager's family first saw it in 1971. It is in this quaint village that the Yeagers created what was to become the Hub Group.

Phil recalled the decision to move:

*It was a crazy move, but I knew Chicago was the best place to go. Even back then, it was known as the intermodal hub, with its location almost literally in the center of the country. I thought I knew more than any of my competitors, since I had a total of 19 years of experience in the railroad, with 12 of those years in intermodal to fall back on. I had helped the railroad for all those years, and now it was going to help me in return. It was going to be a partnership. And it has been a great partnership ever since the beginning.[3]*

Upon arriving in Chicago, the family temporarily settled in a small apartment they rented monthly

---

Hub City Terminals, Inc., began operations on April 19, 1971. The first logo was designed to represent the hub and spokes of a wheel.

at the Mayflower Motel in Clarendon Hills, another railroad suburb a few miles west of Hinsdale. Shortly after moving, Phil started looking for office space for his new business. Through an ad in a local newspaper, he found a small second-story room for rent above a florist shop in Hinsdale, within walking distance of the train station. The rent was $85 a month for the windowless room, which measured 110 square feet, only slighter bigger than an elevator.[4]

The Yeager family in the early 1970s. From left to right: Phil; David, 17; Mark, 6; Debra, 13; and Joyce.

### The Dream Takes Shape

The Yeagers realized $20,000 from the sale of their New Jersey home. They planned to use half the money for the down payment of a house, and earmarked the other half to start the company.

Phil lamented, "That's all we had. So it was a very small beginning, and failure was not a word I could afford."[5]

On April 19, 1971, Hub City Terminals, Inc., officially opened its single door for business. Within a few months, the family found a home in the nearby railroad suburb, Downers Grove, just five miles west of the Hinsdale office. Downers Grove was affordable, offered good schools, and provided a safe and comfortable neighborhood for raising children.[6]

At this time, the Yeager's eldest son, David, attended college at the University of Dayton in Ohio, while their daughter, Debra, and son Mark, attended public school. Trained as a legal secretary, Joyce helped out with the family's fledgling business by working in the windowless office, where she handled the paperwork and managed the business operations, while Phil took to the streets to sell.[7]

Jim Brady, who worked at Southern Pacific Railroad at the time, recalled, "Trailer on flatcar (TOFC) was a new product in the marketplace, but the rail carriers couldn't care less about it. Certain individuals in the freight business, Phil Yeager in particular, saw the opportunity to handle the business as shipper agents."[8]

### A Husband-and-Wife Team

Each morning, when Joyce arrived at the tiny office, Phil headed off to Chicago to make sales calls. Phil recalled:

*For the first three or four months, we just had one desk, so we needed to share it. When Joyce came to work in the morning, I would go out and start making calls on customers as early as 8:30 A.M. I'd walk into the potential customer's office with a few doughnuts and coffee, and sit down and have breakfast with the guy. At the end of the day, I would come back to the office from soliciting, and Joyce would go home so I could use the desk. We were that small of an operation.[9]*

Joyce kept track of all the freight shipments on index cards taped to the wall, and she worked the phones while Phil pounded the pavement.[10] The Yeagers' daughter, Debra, recalled, "They were very excited about building a business together, and they worked very, very hard. They worked constantly, but we spent every evening together as a family. We always ate dinner together, and my mom would help prepare it when she got home. She always kept the family together. She was so organized."[11]

Not surprisingly, Hub was a constant topic of conversation. "Our children heard everything about the business," Phil recalled. "All they heard at home was 'Hub, Hub, Hub.' Finally one day Mark said, 'Why do we always have to talk about Hub?' I tried to explain the importance of our business venture and said, 'Someday, Mark, you will understand.'"[12]

Early on, even the children assisted with the business. On breaks from college, David helped out with the office work. Phil recalled, "When Mark was seven, he became an official employee of Hub City under the direction of his big sister, Debra. His job was polishing the desks and taking out the garbage at a princely rate of $1 a week. After about a year, he came to my office

Below left: The Yeagers' first tiny one-room office was within walking distance of the Hinsdale train station pictured here.

Below right: The Yeagers decided to launch their new business in Hinsdale, a beautiful suburb of Chicago, after making the strategic move from New Jersey.

with a serious look on his face, and asked to speak with me. I knew it was important, so I said, 'Let's talk.' Mark said, 'I've been working for Hub for over a year, and my workload has increased from one desk to several, but my pay is still one buck.' Mark wore me down after some strong negotiations, and I raised his salary to $5 a week."[13]

### Part Salesman, Diplomat, and Ambassador

Shortly after launching the business, Phil realized that he needed a car for work. Because the family finances were so low, Phil could only afford a seven-year-old Volkswagen Beetle. "The floor boards were worn through," Phil explained, "so I put some cardboard there. We used that car for over a year-and-

Above: David Yeager graduated from high school in Cranford, New Jersey, just before his family moved to the Chicago area in 1971.

Below: Both Debra and Mark assisted in the fledgling Hub business by cleaning the office and taking out the trash on weekends. Here, they are pictured taking a break with the family's cat.

a-half. It was a great little car. I paid 500 bucks for it, and I sold it for $500."

Phil made his first calls driving his red VW to contacts he had established while on the railroad side of the business. "The Santa Fe Railroad person in New York called their Chicago office for me and said, 'Phil's coming out there. Let's treat him right. He'll provide us with good business.' He had more confidence in me than I did!" said Phil. Phil's previous business relationship with the company and his networking skills served him well.[20] He explained:

*I lived by my belief: "The harder you work, the luckier you get." I'd be out selling all day. Most salespeople thought four or five calls a day was a lot, but I made 10 or 12 a day or I wasn't happy. Joyce worked 50 hours a week and also took care of the kids, and I worked 70 hours. I got to know all the railroad people in Chicago very quickly, and it proved to be very important. Very important.[14]*

Tom Hardin, Hub's current president of Rail Affairs and the Yeagers' first hire, explained, "There were only five or six of us so-called shipper agents in the business in Chicago at the time, and we had a little network in the area. We would talk late in the day and see who could match freight with whom."[15]

During this period, Hub's business focused on ramp-to-ramp (also known as railroad terminal to terminal) shipments. Hub made arrangements for the movement of cargo from the railroad terminal nearest to its customer to the railroad terminal nearest to the receiver. Hub negotiated volume contracts with the railroads, booking freight containers for its customers. In essence, Hub acted as a third-party shipper for the shipping industry.[16]

To secure better rail prices, shipper agents like Hub needed high volume. Competing shipper agents often had to team up and consolidate their loads to satisfy the two-trailer restriction imposed by the Interstate Commerce Commission (ICC) at the time.[17] The two-trailer restriction meant that shippers were required to pay for and load two trailers at a time. The ICC imposed the restriction

# CHICAGO:
# THE CROSSROADS OF AMERICA

S OME MIGHT ARGUE THAT IT'S NEW YORK or the Eastern Corridor, but according to the venerated Chicago Historical Society, the most important railroad center in North America is ... Chicago.

More lines of track radiate in more directions from the Windy City than from any other place in the United States. It is the hub of the nation's major railroads and the hub for Amtrak, which is America's last remaining intercity rail passenger system. Chicago truly embodies the phrase "crossroads of America."

The history of Chicago's railroads stretches back to 1848, when the Galena & Chicago Union planned to build tracks to the mines in Galena

Now in practically every major city across the nation, Hub's modest start began at the hub of transportation—Chicago.

in northwestern Illinois, and instead, sent them west to a suburb now known as Oak Park. By the latter half of the 19th century, more than 11 railroad lines completed tracks linking Chicago with the wheat fields in Illinois and northern Wisconsin, and every major city in middle America.

Though the nation's railroads have merged into just a few large systems, Chicago remains a hub where the tracks of one company end and those of the next begin.[1]

because each railroad flatcar carried two trailers, and the railroads wanted to ensure that each flatcar was full.

When he worked for the railroad, Phil learned how to deal with shipper agents from the railroad side. Now, working as a shipper agent, Phil knew the perspective of people who worked for the railroad, and he knew how to gain their trust. Phil said:

*There were only about 40 shipper agents in the entire country. I had a number of contacts with the railroads, individuals who liked me personally. That, coupled with my many years of expe-*

*rience working for the railroad, helped develop our initial shipper agent business.*[18]

Phil's reputation helped him overcome the prejudice many in the transportation industry felt toward shipper agents. "The railroads hated the idea of shipper agents," Phil said. "They didn't want to use them. They were trying to provide the services themselves. There was a lot of mistrust and hostility."[19]

Though the railroads made changes that hurt shipper agents' credibility with customers, shipper agents could still arrange to move freight faster and more efficiently than the shippers could themselves. Phil set out to change the impression of shipper agents as cutthroats and convince the freight transportation industry that using shipper agents was the wave of the future. "I believe that I was the first shipper agent with railroad experience. I was sincere and truthful, and I knew the good and bad of the railroads. I had a broad view of both the railroad and the shipper agent industry. This was my future, and I was going to do it right. I don't want to brag about it, but in hindsight, I was certainly one of the people who first brought the railroads and shipper's agents together."[20] Hardin agreed:

> *Phil gave real credibility to the industry. People knew who Phil Yeager was nationally. He brought a reputation and a great customer following from his days with the Penn Central.*[21]

Phil's good reputation helped convince shippers to use Hub. Yet, for all his tenacity, Phil still wasn't signing large accounts. By September 1971, only more than four months after beginning Hub City Terminals, Inc., the company came close to bankruptcy. Phil said, "Fortunately,

we had some cash flow from our early customers, but we didn't start off with a boom. It was a very hard process. I didn't get a lot from the bigger companies. It was the smaller ones that kept us going, along with the good reputation I had built up with the railroads."[22]

### The Nabisco Advantage

Phil's big break came as a result of his connections at Nabisco, the renowned baking and snack company. For years, he had interacted with executives there in his capacity as assistant director of intermodal at the Pennsylvania Railroad. At the time, Nabisco distrusted shipper agents—as many companies did—and Phil had only managed to procure irregular shipment orders from the company. Then, one day, Phil received a call from Don Maltby, Sr., an old contact of his and an executive with Nabisco. Phil said, "He called me because he couldn't get an interchange agreement for his trucking company to get trailers with the Rock Island Railroad. I said, 'I'll do it. How much time do I have?' and he said, 'No time; get those trailers right now.' I said, 'I'll call you back in 20 minutes.' "[23]

# NABISCO AND HUB:
# A LASTING RELATIONSHIP

NABISCO TRANSPORTATION executive Don Maltby, Sr., called on Phillip Yeager at Hub in the fall of 1971. "I had a feeling that we could save a considerable amount of money by shipping by piggyback," he recalled.

But Nabisco, like many large companies in the early 1970s, remained staunchly anti-piggyback. At that time, American businesses shipped the majority of freight by truck. Maltby explained:

> *They had the feeling that a truck would leave on Monday and be there on Tuesday.*

*They literally thought things would be sidetracked by using the railroad; that we'd have a tremendous amount of damage because of the extra handling that's involved in piggyback. We had to overcome that mentality.*

At Maltby's urging, Nabisco finally decided to give Hub a try. After successfully handling the first challenge from Nabisco, Hub got a second order and then a third. Maltby said, "We recorded every shipment for the first two or three months on this program. The records revealed that working through Hub made

Phil knew he could get the job done because of his long-standing relationship with the terminal manager for the Rock Island Railroad. Phil continued, "So I called the terminal manager and said, 'I need an interchange for Nabisco, and they've got a lot of freight, and you're going to get in on it.' The terminal manager knew a good opportunity when it came his way, and he knew he could trust me. He said, 'Sure, you've got it, come get the trailers, and I said, 'When?' and he said, 'Now.' "[24]

The shipment started going out that same day, on a Friday, and by Monday, Nabisco had 30 loads of freight at its doorstep. The movement had gone out as promised and arrived on time. "It cemented my business relationship with Nabisco," Phil said. "It established Hub as a leader in the industry and gave us credibility with other big shippers. Due to that one event, our business tripled."[25] By the end of Hub's first year in business, the company had moved 900 trailers, and the business continued to grow rapidly. After four years, Hub became the largest shipper agent in the country.[26]

Along with the growing business and continued success came the need to bring in some outside help. Phil recalled:

great financial sense. Management was satisfied and said, 'Yes, this looks like a good deal, let's explore it a little further.' "

Thirty-five years later, Hub continues to move product for Nabisco (now part of Kraft Foods), and it successfully meets every shipping challenge. Today, the two business giants enjoy a mutually beneficial relationship.

Reflecting on the long-term relationship between Hub and Nabisco, Maltby said, "Phil was a terrific railroad man, and he had the sense of adventure to see this potential with a new way of shipping product. He felt that with the cooperation of the cartage companies and the select railroads that he was doing business with, that he could pull this thing off. He also could give the customer an economic windfall, and yet still maintain a good degree of service."[1]

*Joyce and I were working so hard. Finally, I came home and I said, "We've got to do something. I've got to get the best person in Chicago. I don't want any seconds here." She said, "I know who we should hire. He's the only guy for us. His name is Tom Hardin."*[27]

**Hardin Makes Three**

Tom Hardin operated a small shipper agent business when he first met the Yeagers in 1971. "I actually got to know Joyce first because of the old model of our business," Hardin remembered. "In the old days, you had to collaborate and combine shipments in order to make the volume requirements. Joyce and I became friends, and we worked very well together. I guess that's why Joyce recommended me to Phil. When he first called me, my initial reaction was, 'You're the new guy.' I ran the third largest shipper agent business in Chicago, and we'd been in business 10 years. So I put him off a couple of times."[28] But Phil persisted. He finally persuaded Hardin to come to lunch. Phil said, "I asked Hardin how much business he was handling. He said, '300 trailers a month,' and then I said to him, 'Well, I've been in business six months, and I'm handling that and more.' "[29]

After lunch, Phil took Hardin up to his tiny office. Hub was still atop the flower shop, but it had grown to include an adjacent office—albeit another room without a window. Hardin said, "He opened up the books to me and, lo and behold, he was probably moving at least twice the business we were, even with our 10-year head start. And it was just the two of them, he and Joyce. I thought we could work well together. I knew his background with the railroad, which was the same as mine. We were unique in our business backgrounds compared to our competitors." Hardin continued:

*The shipper agent business was rough-and-tumble. It was mostly made up of guys who owned local trucking companies and took advantage of railroads. The railroads needed a catalyst to go out and bring them intermodal business. They didn't want to hire their own sales force, but they didn't trust the majority of shipper agents, either.*

*Most shipper agents were a bunch of loose-knit operators. The guys didn't have an understanding of what the railroads needed. They were governed by their own quick-hit needs. Both Phil and I understood the big picture from the railroad perspective. We knew how to provide good service, these local guys didn't. I saw that Phil was the right match for me, and I think he saw that I was right for him.*[30]

Together, Hardin knew he and Phil would make a winning team, so he accepted Phil's offer to become Hub's first official employee. Phil explained, "I was pretty straight-laced. I told him, 'If you're coming with me, I don't want you to bring any account information. I want you to tell your accounts, the ones you feel are your good friends, that you're going with me, but that you can't handle their business for a year.'"[31]

"I knew this was the right guy," Hardin said. "It was the right thing to do. We shook hands, and I came to work for Hub." When the year was up,

the majority of Hardin's former clients followed him to the fastest-growing shipper agent business in the country, Hub.[32]

### The Ship-a-Train Program

At the tail end of 1972, Phil's contacts with the railroads once again brought tiny Hub City Terminals, Inc., an opportunity that would prove to be invaluable to its business. Phil received a call from his former employer, the Penn Central. The railroad was losing a great deal of shipping business in its northeast corridor to over-the-road trucking companies. To compete with the truckers, Penn Central required Hub City to ship 60 trailers, twice a week, from Chicago to New York. As part of the deal, Hub had to take the trailers on a "take or pay" basis. This meant that Hub needed to pay for the 60 spots on

# "SHIP-A-TRAIN" TAKES OFF

DECEMBER 1972. HUB CITY TERMINALS, Inc., agrees to an unprecedented "take or pay" deal with the Penn Central. They must pay for 60 trailers or containers, headed to New York from Chicago, twice a week, whether they are filled with customer's goods or not. Tom Hardin recalled, "The very first day we opened for business with the railroad, Phil, Ray Axelstrom (Hub's second employee), and I actually went down to the terminal to check on the shipments and coordinate with the rail people. We were very, very nervous."[1] That first day brought them good luck. Phil Yeager explained, "On the first train, we had 55 trailers and containers. The break-even point was 53, so we made a little money."[2]

But the second day was a different story. Hub sold only 23 of the necessary 60. "We lost about $15,000. This was at a time when we did not even have $15,000. But, thankfully, the trains caught on," Phil said.[3]

Shortly thereafter, the other railroads competed by offering 10-trailer rates at the same prices. Instead of panicking, Hub took on the competition and managed to develop an entire market out of its

flagship program. "The market for us actually expanded when the competition came," Phil said.[4]

Happy with the success of the initial Ship-a-Train program, the Penn Central expanded it into Boston, Philadelphia, and Baltimore; and the Norfolk & Western (N&W) Railroad offered a similar program into Norfolk.

In four short years, Hub grew from handling 3,000 to 4,000 trailers a year to becoming the largest shipper agent in the country. Phil explained the impact this program had on his business:

*We became the largest shipper agent mostly on the basis of these trains. In fact, about 75 percent of our business went East. This built our reputation. It gave us a good image, not only to the railroads but to the big shippers and the small shippers as well.*[5]

Phil's solitary employee at the time, Hardin, made this point, "In my opinion, the Ship-a-Train program was *the* most important event in Hub's history."[6]

the train whether they sold the business that would fill them or not. In return, Penn Central offered Hub exclusive, favorable rates. They would call it the Ship-a-Train program.

"At that time, we were probably handling between 20 and 30 trailers and containers a month between Chicago and New York," Phil said. "But I knew this could work. I just had that feeling. I knew the volume potential was there because of my experience on the railroad."[33] Hub decided to go for it. Hardin concurred, "It was a landmark decision on our part to go into that agreement with them. We knew we had the pricing that was competitive enough to give us an advantage against the over-the-road trucking companies, but obviously we had to go out there and secure the business. The clock was ticking."[34]

Phil's business contacts and sales acumen again paid off, and he quickly sold space to customers eager to take advantage of such low rates. "We just got in there, and we built that train in a very short period of time," Phil recalled.[35] Hub almost always met the minimum trailer requirements, and the success of the program helped it grow to a point where Hub shipped more than 120 trailers a day.

Because of Hub's exclusive rates and contract, the company even began arranging shipping for their competitors. Hardin explained:

> It was a great service, and everybody wanted to partake in it. Then we opened up other cities. So actually, it was the springboard for Hub becoming a major national transportation entity.
>
> The success of Ship-a-Train gave us a shot of confidence and also gave us a lot of publicity in the Chicago area. We were the first ones getting into the market from Chicago, and we dominated movement into the East. We were the largest intermodal shipper on each of the railroads in the East during that period.[36]

In the freight-shipping business, volume is key. Railroads pay attention to large customers, and with the Ship-a-Train program, Hub became a large and important customer to the railroads overnight.

### From Florist to Laundry

By 1973, the tiny offices of Hub City Terminals, Inc., were bursting at the seams with six employees.

Hardin remembered, "It was busy day and night. I would have two telephones going at once. Joyce answered phones and typed invoices, in addition to doing all the accounting work. The hours were long, and the space was small and cramped. It was time to move."

The company found space above a laundry in nearby Clarendon Hills. Hardin recalled:

> I got an office with a window. I thought, "Wow, life is good." That was a great move. I felt that we were really growing. This was going to be a permanent business.[37]

Phil concurred, "We were just amazed at all this space. We could actually fit in all our furniture. The office had lots of windows. That was a big deal."[38]

Phil's strong work ethic and growing business gained attention from the railroad industry. Ron Hazlett, regional manager of intermodal for the Illinois Central Railroad at the time, recalled his first impression of Phil. "First of all, he called on me. Here comes this big, tall, good-looking, well-dressed guy into my office. He introduced himself and had some information about his company for me. That was unusual. He was *my* customer, but there he was calling on me. He gave me his rate sheet. I was amazed. 'I should be calling on him,' I thought. At the time, I was surprised, but in retrospect, I realized he was a smart businessman who was building up the trust and confidence of the railroad."[39]

Not long after their meeting, Hazlett received another surprise. "Tom and Phil invited me to lunch. I was the carrier, I should have bought them lunch," Hazlett said. "But I agreed to go." At the lunch, Phil, who still handled all the sales himself, offered Hazlett a job in sales with Hub. Phil guaranteed Hazlett's salary for the first six months, but thereafter he expected Hazlett to work on commission. "Actually, that's what really excited me," Hazlett said, "I had enough confidence that I thought I could make a lot of money on commission. Of course, being the first salesman [other than Phil] in Chicago selling intermodal for Hub was also an incentive. Anything in the city of Chicago was my territory. So I jumped at it." Four months later, Hazlett begged to come off salary and go on to straight commission. "Phil tried to talk me out of it, but I said, 'No, I'd rather do it now,' and that turned out to be a good decision."[40]

Another early Hub hire was George Olson. Olson said:

*I knew Phil because I'd worked for the Pennsylvania Railroad years before. Before I joined Hub in 1975, I was working for another small shipper agent. All the other agents were kind of afraid of Phil. I think they knew he was going to be a strong competitor when he came to town, because he knew what he was doing. So it kind of put fear in everyone's hearts when he set up shop. There were only about 16 people in the whole organization when I joined.*[41]

Olson held a variety of positions with the company, the last being manager of fleet operations when he retired in 2001. "I worked for Hub for 26 years, and I think that says it all. If I didn't think that they were great people, I certainly would not have lasted that long," Olson said.[42]

Although Hub continued to grow, many of the railroads that relied on it to keep their assets full lost business to the trucking industry and other forms of freight transportation. The ICC's tight regulations, an excess of railroad companies competing for the shrinking business, and costly maintenance of routes had all taken their toll on the railroad industry. Many of the railroads merged, ripped up track, or sought bankruptcy protection in their fight for survival.[43]

On the other hand, Hub was doing so well selling their services that, by 1974, Phil had traded in the Volkswagen with the rusted-out floorboards for another company car. This was a much more impressive and much larger Oldsmobile 88. Phil recalled an incident surrounding the new addition shortly after purchasing the car. A Hub client from Chicago came to the office and, after taking a look at the new impressive company car, commented to Phil, "Which half did we buy?" Phil recalled, "I said, 'You didn't buy either half. Hub bought it.'" Not long after, Phil returned from a sales trip to discover that the client had canceled half of his routing schedule with Hub. Phil said, "I learned something there. We didn't bring new cars around customers for a long, long, long time."[44]

### Hub Buys a Building

With Hub's business success, it soon outgrew the second-floor offices over the laundry. "We practically stacked people in there," Phil said. "It was awful. Thankfully, the fellow who owned the laundry business said he would rent me the first floor if I was interested. I said, 'How about selling me the whole building?' and he did, so we moved downstairs as well. After we took over the building, we could accommodate 25 people on the two floors. We needed it. We were growing so fast."[45] Hardin concurred, "Buying the building was a watershed event. We had our own stand-alone business with our name on it. It felt great. I couldn't imagine it could get any better than that."[46]

George Woodward, who served as Conrail's vice president of intermodal and is current president of the University of Denver's Intermodal Transportation Institute (ITI), explained what he viewed as the key to Hub's success:

*One of the real impediments to developing a national network of intermodal was the fact that the rail industry was so fragmented at the time. We had a number of major carriers in the United States, and none of them could grasp the concept of putting together a national network and retailing the services directly to the shipping public.*

*The real innovation came from Phil Yeager, who understood that he could put together a national network, put the railroads behind the scenes, and then create—what appeared to the shipping public—an integrated intermodal product.*[47]

### All in the Family

Phil's oldest son, David, who had been working part-time during the summers for the company while attending college, decided to join the company in 1975. David explained:

*I swore I'd never work for my father. But right before I graduated, my father called me up and said that one of our guys was leaving. I had worked three summers there, so I knew the business, and I'd subbed for probably half of the operations staff. It was the only job offer I had, so I took it. I asked him during that phone call, "When do you want me to start?" He asked, "Well, when do you graduate?"and I said, "Saturday." He said, "Good. Be here on Monday at 8 A.M." And I was. He paid me a whopping sum of about $6,000 a year, and he* *didn't understand why I couldn't afford to move out of the house when I first moved back.*[48]

Phil's frugal sensibilities extended beyond David's salary. "One of his famous lines was, 'Don't buy an electric pencil sharpener. You can do it yourself; and he still has his first hand-held pencil sharpener," recalled his youngest son, Mark, who would later join the company. "Dad is very, very financially conservative, very debt adverse. He really just wants to make sure you're making money before you go out and spend it."[49]

Hub City Terminals, Inc.'s, financial health benefited from Phil's policy of fiscal responsibility. By the time David joined the company, it had grown from $300,000 in sales its first year, to more than $20 million in sales in 1975, with an intermodal network stretching all across the United States.[50] But the company would experience even greater financial success and expansion in the near future. The Yeagers were about to take the company in an entirely new direction and would be rewarded with even more explosive growth.

Joyce, Phil, Mark, and Debra Yeager in a 1978 family photograph. At the time, older brother, David, lived in Pittsburgh where he worked to establish a new hub for the company.

# CHAPTER THREE

# MAJOR EXPANSION

## 1976–1984

*Our greatest asset is our people. They are the best in the intermodal industry. They always have been and always will be.*

—Phillip Yeager

IN 1975, APPROXIMATELY 50 SHIP-per agencies existed like Hub City Terminals, Inc.; by 1985, there were more than 600. The intermodal industry saw striking changes in the years in between that would set the stage for explosive growth for all shipper agents. Hub, along with other shipper agents, continued to grow by leaps and bounds. Phillip Yeager explained, "I was traveling a lot, but I just couldn't seem to keep up with all the potential business." The addition of Ron Hazlett, as Hub's first salesman, had helped with the Chicago-area market, but now the Yeagers believed a second office in another freight center would help them expand their business.[1]

To do that, the Yeagers came up with a novel approach to attract intermodal talent. "We decided to create a series of Subchapter S corporations, named after a section of the tax code that made starting a corporation a desirable way of launching a business," Phil said.[2] Subchapter S is an IRS regulation that gives a corporation with 35 or fewer shareholders the option of being taxed as a partnership to escape corporate income taxes. The net profit or loss from the company is simply divided among the shareholders based on the percentage of ownership.[3] "The Subchapter S corporation was the right way to go because you distributed the company's profits at the end of the year based on ownership," Tom Hardin said. "It

was a great incentive on both ends. It made me care about the well-being of every Subchapter S corporation in the business, as well as Hub Chicago. It was really the kind of magic bullet that brought everybody together."[4]

Phil decided to approach entrepreneurs, preferably with railroad experience, and ask them to invest anywhere from $20,000 to $30,000 in order to become president or principal of a local Subchapter S corporation or Hub Operating Company, as it was referred to at the time. In return, each investor received 25 percent of the stock in his individual corporation.[5] In addition, Phil and other key Hub employees purchased an ownership stake in the hub.[6] Phil commented:

*We selected individuals who we thought had a lot of guts, a lot of confidence in themselves, who were ready to take the chance. We brought in people who perhaps had not succeeded as well with their own companies as they thought they should. You've got to have drive to do something like this—especially when you're starting*

Phil and Joyce Yeager—the original husband-and-wife team and model for the couples that would open 15 of the first Subchapter S companies—shown during a rare vacation in 1984.

*out—and all of these companies were started with very low capital. Some of these guys couldn't have gotten into it otherwise. Just like me, the money they put in was all they had. They had to succeed.*[7]

Phil and Hardin offered Hub Operating Company positions to many of their established associates. "We knew our business. We went from our gut, and we knew how to evaluate the right person for the job," Hardin said. They decided to seek out young husband-and-wife teams like Phil and Joyce, eager to make their mark in the business world.

Wisely, they decided to base those hubs in cities with large shipping centers. The Yeagers chose to model the new hubs after the one Phil and Joyce first created in Chicago. Offices would be small, with little more than a desk and a tele-

# Ron Hazlett

R ON HAZLETT STARTED HIS CAREER IN transportation as chief clerk at the Chicago and Eastern Railroad in 1959. He moved on to sales positions in Minneapolis, Cedar Rapids, Chicago, Memphis, and New York City. In 1969, Hazlett accepted a position as the Midwest manager of intermodal with the Illinois Central Railroad in Chicago.

Recognizing Hazlett's strong business capabilities, Phil Yeager hired him as Hub City Terminals' first sales manager in 1973. Hazlett opened Hub City North Central in Milwaukee in 1976 and stayed there until his retirement in 1997. According to Phil, "Ron was not only a good salesman, he was also known for his management and shrewd negotiating skills, and his competitive nature. He just couldn't stand losing a piece of business to a competitor."[1]

phone. Husbands, with the title of "president," would make the sales calls; wives, with the title of "vice president," would do the paperwork and manage the operations.[8] The Mr. Outside–Mrs. Inside formula, as the Yeagers sometimes called it, proved extremely successful for Chicago, and would for the subsequent hubs.[9]

After finding the right husband-and-wife team to head it, each hub would have almost complete autonomy. "I didn't want any Indians. I love chiefs, and by chiefs I mean decision makers," Phil said.

### The First Hub Operating Companies

Yeager chose Detroit as the first city for a hub outside of Chicago, and less than a year later opened a third hub in nearby Milwaukee.[10] Though only 90 minutes from Chicago, this office, as the base for the North Central hub, would help cement the company's dominance in the Midwest and eventually all of Wisconsin, Minnesota, and North and South Dakota. Phil offered Hazlett, Hub's first salesman, the new assignment, and he eagerly accepted it. Hazlett explained:

*I was doing so well as a salesman that I leapt at the opportunity. Most people with a growing company would create subsidiaries with separate offices, and certainly wouldn't offer an ownership stake. But Phil always offered that opportunity. I think with Milwaukee, I actually kicked in more than 25 percent of the start-up cost, because I was that excited. Of course, the ownership stake did two things. It kept you awake at night if you weren't making money, and it made you smile an awful lot when you did.*[11]

Hazlett and his wife moved to Milwaukee in the summer of 1976, and he remained with Hub until his retirement in 1997. Hazlett recalled about Phil: "I don't think I ever had a written contract with Phil personally. It was all done with a handshake. I mean, his integrity was beyond belief. He was aboveboard, honest. He was never greedy, and he made a lot of people very wealthy. But it was always a joke with Phil because he was very insistent, very nervous about any kind of debt. He would make his own collection calls. He watched the books. He wanted to make sure that the company was not going to go bankrupt under his leadership. When I was in Milwaukee and owed him money, he'd call me and say I'd better get a check down to him. We're partners, and we're friends and everything else, but I'd better get that check to him."[12]

### A Key Railroad Merger

During 1975, while Hub began to create its network, there were approximately 75 major railroads operating in the United States (by 2006, there would be just four). As the railroads fought to keep ahead of economic woes, several merged to stave off bankruptcy and to compete through consolidation. On April 1, 1976, a consortium of six railroads operating in the eastern portion of America were folded into the Consolidated Rail Corporation, or Conrail. Hardin recalled the effect this had on Hub business:

*They became extremely difficult to do business with. It was their way or the highway—kind of figuratively and literally. Many of the railroads at that time were going through a huge cost-cutting process in order to stay alive and, of course, those things are always painful for the customer. Conrail was the first one of those, and that emerged into essentially a very efficient monopoly, which was unique in the industry. That was the first big one that we really felt.*

But the extensive railroad background of Phil and Hardin, as well as new Hub hires, would help make relationships with the newly merged railroads profitable—even one as rigid as Conrail. "We did well with them," Hardin said, "As they got larger, they identified their needs, and we did well. We worked really hard at that relationship. We became a good partner and worked through the difficulties. That's always been our history."[13]

### The Family Connection

Phil's son David joined Hub in 1975. During his first two years with the company, David performed a variety of duties in the office. "I don't even remem-

Above: Phil Yeager demonstrates the power of hard work with son Mark in this family snapshot taken after a typical midwestern snowstorm.

Below: A determined David Yeager and future wife, Julia, got their feet wet when they opened a Hub Operating Company in the tough-to-crack city of Pittsburgh during an economic downturn in 1978.

ber all that I did. I'd take calls from customers and then call in billing to railroads because there were no fax machines at that point," David said.

By 1977, David decided it was time to jump into sales. "So I started calling on both international and domestic customers. In the year that followed, I thought I knew everything there was to know for a 25-year-old, so I decided it was time for me to open up and run one of the new Hub Operating Companies." After discussing with his father the pros and cons of starting a company on the West Coast or in Pittsburgh, David, at his father's suggestion, opted for the latter. "Being the naive kid that I was, I chose to go to Pittsburgh, Pennsylvania," David recalled. So in April 1978, David and his fiancée, Julia Troppoli, headed for their new assignment in Pittsburgh. David quickly realized that he'd taken on a very challenging responsibility.[14]

Above: A formal portrait of the Yeager family at their Downers Grove, Illinois, home in 1978. Left to right: Mark, Debra, David, Joyce, and Phil. *(Portrait by Worline Studio.)*

Left: Richard and Thelma Merrill served as president and vice president of Hub City New Haven, Connecticut, starting in 1978. Their son, Chris, would join Hub in 1984.

"At the time, launching a business in Pittsburgh was really rough. I mean, it was just brutal. We hit it right during the steel recession. So we went in there when many businesses were already in decline. It was a very difficult time. But somehow, we did manage to eke out a profit, though it wasn't overwhelming."[15]

While David persevered in Pittsburgh, Hub continued to expand into new territories. Between 1978 and 1980 it opened hubs in Boston, Toledo, and New Haven. Richard and Thelma Merrill opened the Connecticut office in 1978. Chris Merrill, a second-generation Hub employee (currently sales manager of the northeast region out of Hub Boston) recalled this period:

*Dad's was the fifth office in the Hub chain. My mother and father ran the office, and at first, they ran it out of our house, like a lot of those had started. When I got home from college on break, they'd say, "Just answer the phone, Hub City, and tell the customers we'll be right with them." Little did I know, I would make this my career.*

*I would say the most important piece of advice my dad gave me when I started working for Hub in 1984 was to remember who the customer is, and to always value a good customer—be loyal, be truthful—and remember that service is number one. That's what we sell at Hub Group. That's what we provide. That's where we excel. Without that, we wouldn't differentiate ourselves from anyone else. That comes directly from Phillip Yeager's leadership.*[16]

Phil's son David was also learning those lessons during his stint heading up the Pittsburgh Hub along with his new wife, Julia. During a routine sales call, David met Ed Peterson, the man who would later take his place in Pittsburgh. Peterson recalled the circumstances, "After working for the Canadian Pacific Railroad, I joined a consumer goods company in 1979. Dave came to call on me soliciting business from Michigan out to California via intermodal, which I was glad to give him because it was much cheaper than the truckload carriers that we were using. That was my first exposure to intermodal."

The two men hit it off, and shortly thereafter, Peterson got a surprising call from David. Peterson explained:

*He said that he was moving to St. Louis. They had an office there that had some issues, and he was going to try to fix it. He was looking for somebody to take over Pittsburgh, and he thought I might be the right candidate. So he offered it to me, and I turned him down. He offered it again, and I turned it down. On the third go-around, I decided well, okay, why not? It took a little convincing, because Pittsburgh was a very modest undertaking as I saw it. I had a career path that was pretty well established, and this would be more a leap of faith than anything. But I knew I was young enough to recover from a mistake, and it looked like a heck of an opportunity. I was anxious to find a challenge like that.*[17]

Peterson took the leap of faith. He and his wife, Cindy, followed the husband-and-wife team approach that was working so successfully for Hub. Peterson recalled, "I hired a guy, and he ran the office when I went out and sold, but then at night, my wife and I would do all the correspondence and the invoicing, and things like that. We did that for years and years. I mean we worked hard—16 hours a day, six days a week. Sunday might have been a day of rest for some people, but we were getting ready for Monday. I'd write checks in the morning. We'd get the checkbook down to under five bucks, then I quit writing the checks. That's how tight it was sometimes."[18]

Peterson's perseverance paid off when he landed a large account in 1981. "It was the first decent sale that I made," he said. "It convinced me that I could do this because, quite frankly, I didn't know the product that well when I took over in 1980. I knew it from a buyer's point of view, so I had to learn the product. I didn't have any background in accounting or bookkeeping, and I was all tan-

Beginning in the early 1980s, Hub assembled its extended family each year for annual gatherings that combined business with pleasure. Pictured here are Ed Peterson and wife, Cindy, who replaced David Yeager in heading the Pittsburgh office.

gled up with all those details as well. It was a very steep learning curve."

The Pittsburgh hub would go on to become a great financial success for the company. Peterson is quick to point to Phil's business wizardry as a reason for that success. He commented:

*Phil did something that was so unique and so unusual, and is easily overlooked. That is, he created a structure that just created success. What this man did was he would walk around with his magic wand and tap people on the shoulder. I'm quite serious. He would literally, in a metaphorical sense, put his hand on your shoulder, and he'd turn you into a millionaire. He put a structure in place that just bred success. He told you what he wanted you to do, and then he got out of your way. There was no micromanagement. He had faith in your ability to succeed. And it worked like a charm almost every time, and that's the story of Hub. I'll tell you—Hub is entrepreneurship at its very best.[19]*

Meanwhile, David and Julia Yeager had headed back to the Midwest to take over the St. Louis hub in 1980. David found the assignment to his liking after rough-and-tumble Pittsburgh. David explained:

*Even though there was more competition from shipper agents in St. Louis as opposed to Pittsburgh, it was much more of a country club environment. After being trained by a bunch of pit bulls in Pittsburgh, we took off pretty aggressively in St. Louis. Within a year, we became the largest shipper agent in the area.*

Shortly after David launched Hub City St. Louis, another member of the Yeager family—this time Phil's son-in-law, Robert Jensen—would join Hub. Jensen and Phil's daughter, Debra, met while attending the University of Illinois in the mid-1970s. Jensen remembers his first visit to the Hub offices: "Debra and I were dating at the time, and I remember stopping by the office to pick her up. Her parents still expected her to clean the office! So I went there to help her vacuum and clean up. That was in 1975."

After the couple graduated from college, they married, and Jensen pursued a career in finance before accepting an offer from Phil to come to work for Hub St. Louis. "When I joined Hub, I did everything

from making the coffee to posting the transactions. I literally did everything except for sales," Jensen recalled. "Then, around 1983, my brother-in-law, David, who was president at the time, left St. Louis to go to Chicago, and I was named president."[20]

Emulating the husband-and-wife business model created by Phil and Joyce, Debra worked in operations next to her husband. Debra explained:

*It was a new adventure. I had never worked with my husband, so it was a nice opportunity, and it was a lot of fun. I used to take my youngest one with me to the office and put him behind my desk, and he'd sleep while I worked on payroll. I thought it was going to be tough, working for dad, but both Robert and I liked it.[21]*

Below: Hub outgrew its second office in Clarendon Hills during the 1980s. Phil Yeager then bought this one in Downers Grove, another of Chicago's western "train" suburbs.

Inset: Moving day.

### South of the Border

As they continued to grow Hub, Phil and Hardin used their instincts and relied on their contacts and experience to select the right executive to run each new hub. Hardin said, "What we were doing with the hub expansion was finding the best person first, and if we were both in agreement that the person had the skill sets that we needed, we'd make an approach. We'd have lunch and make our proposition. In addition to the 25-percent investment stake and the title of president, we'd offer a 10-percent bonus of the hub's profits off the top. We didn't offer a big salary. We believed in the incentive approach. We'd pay a $40,000 salary, but offer the ability to make $200,000 a year. The good guys did it. They took their chance."[22]

One man who took a chance was Tom Holzmann. He worked as the director of intermodal sales and service for the Missouri Pacific Railroad, and had been acquainted with Phil and Joyce since 1972. Phil approached Holzmann in June 1980 and asked him to head up a new hub in San Antonio, Texas. Phil wanted Holzmann to introduce Hub to the Mexican marketplace.

As a result, Holzmann needed to establish intermodal movement into and out of Mexico by rail. He explained:

*We were the first company that did that. I had to build up and start the business from scratch. Not only was our company new, but intermodal was new. A lot of people were comfortable only using trucks. So it was a challenge to get the customers, to get the brokers, to get the U.S. side and the Mexican side working together so that they had confidence in the intermodal business. The deregulation to come certainly helped.*

The leadership example set by Phil also helped. Decades later, Holzmann reflected on the success of his division, "Phil Yeager, as founder and leader, has been an inspiration to most of us who opened subsequent hub offices, and who followed in his and Joyce's initial footsteps. His leadership, guidance, and support gave us the encouragement we needed to get our own operations going in a positive direction. For this, we can be forever thankful. It has also been my pleasure to have watched his sons, David and Mark, grow and succeed, and develop their own ideas for the future of today's Hub Group."[23]

### Hub Goes West

As Hub continued to spread its services throughout the Midwest, Phil planned to cultivate a market nationwide that included the West Coast. Hardin recalled, "At one point, Phil said, 'Have you met Bill Schmidt with the Western Pacific Railroad? He's a sharp guy, a great salesman. He lives in San Francisco. I've been talking to him about working for us, and potentially opening a hub on the West Coast.' I said, 'Yeah, I think he's a great guy. Let's talk to him.' That's how we opened Golden Gate, which became one of the most successful hubs."[24]

"Phil wanted Hub to become more of a nationwide company versus just a Chicago- and Midwest-focused company. Phil had been talking with me about the possibility of opening up the company out on the West Coast, San Francisco and so forth. But, at that time, I was completely satisfied working for the railroad," Schmidt explained. "Then, when we learned that the Staggers Rail Act was coming along—this was in early 1980—everyone knew this was going to really revolutionize the way railroads would do business," said Schmidt. The Staggers Rail Act would allow for contracts from a pricing and a customer standpoint. It would permit individual railroads to set their own rate structures rather than going through all the tariff bureaus. "Prior to Staggers, everybody belonged to a rate bureau and everybody had the same rates and processes. The Staggers Rail Act was going to transform the industry. Also, the Western Pacific Railroad planned to consolidate, and I was told that I would be sent to Omaha. I didn't want to go there. So the timing was right. I just felt that working for Phil and Tom would be a great opportunity," said Schmidt.[25]

So, in October 1980, Schmidt set up the Golden Gate office. Schmidt recalled:

*We were the first company in the West, that is, west of Chicago. If 24 hours a day, seven days a week, was supposed to be enough energy and time, it just wasn't. I knew a lot of shippers and their companies. Many East Coast companies had West Coast regional transportation offices, too.*

# HUB AND THE RAILROADS: PARALLEL TRACKS

THE GROWTH OF HUB GROUP COR-relates to the enormous changes that occurred in America's railroad system with the introduction of the Staggers Rail Act in 1980. Up to that time, there were nearly 75 major railroads in the country but most were near bankruptcy. The railroads were experiencing economic woes caused by the increase in highway competition and stringent regulations imposed on the railroad.

But deregulation would change all this. Massive consolidation would occur over the next 30 years. By 2006, only a handful of major U.S. railroads remained in operation. "Both the consolidation and the deregulation of the rail industry was a definite boon to Hub," Tom Hardin stated. "The consolidation of the railroads mirrored the path of Hub's growth. Both were the cause of it and both were benefactors of it. We grew as the railroads grew. We became a bigger player as they grew in size."

Key to that growth was Phil Yeager and Tom Hardin's practice of hiring principals with railroad experience and working closely with the railroad—through thick and thin—in an effort to mutually promote intermodal transportation. Hardin said, "As we became bigger, we developed stronger relationships and better programs that helped put Hub at the top of the heap." As the railroads grew in size and built more fluid networks, they offered clients more options, which in turn allowed Hub to sell a broader range of products and services.

---

Early Golden Gate customers included Del Monte, Sun Diamond Growers, California Almond Exchange, Sierra Pacific Industries, and Kaiser Refractories. "There were an awful lot of small companies that really helped us establish ourselves," he said.

Schmidt found he encountered challenges unique to the West Coast. "Phil recognized that Hub had no presence whatsoever west of Chicago, and when we got over the Rocky Mountains, it was like you could have been in Asia. Right at the beginning, as I was out driving up and down every road and highway trying to call on every building and plant that I could find, I kept sensing something I had a hard time grasping. But over a period of time, it dawned on me," Schmidt said.[26]

He realized that Northern and Southern California have completely different products and types of businesses, so each area requires different transportation needs. Schmidt also found that many of the western companies used trucking companies and ignored intermodal piggyback transportation. Because of the Interstate Commerce Commission's (ICC) long-standing and stringent regulations, many

Bill Schmidt left the Western Pacific Railroad to open up the Golden Gate Hub with his wife, JoAnn.

Though several of the large railroad mergers proved extremely challenging from a service standpoint, the mergers benefited the entire intermodal industry in the long run. Hub's strategy, according to Hardin, "is not to go all in, as one would say, with any one railroad. We want to work with all of the railroads because we need all of their capacity to fuel our growth."

The ongoing partnership between Hub Group and the railroads has no end in sight. Hardin said, "Today's railroad numbers have never been healthier … cash flows are phenomenal and the railroads are able to put a lot of capital back in the system. These kinds of investments are able to create more line capacity." In order to continue to make rail systems attractive to freight customers, the railroads will largely invest in upgrading and making their systems even more efficient. "It's rather mind-boggling that we can do business at the speed of light and literally move millions of loads of freight with very little human intervention," Hardin commented. "So it's the systems that have become more efficient for Hub and for the railroads; they're built for each other and are very integrated."

According to Hardin, possible future technology advancements for the rail systems that would increase efficiency include the development of a 57-foot container (53 feet is now the industry standard) and perhaps, even a more efficient stack railcar. "It's not on the horizon right now," Hardin said. "But I think some day that will happen. Clearly, advancements would need to occur from an engineering standpoint. Either way, I think that by the end of this decade, there might be a transcontinental merger."

No matter what the future brings in terms of efficiency and innovation, the relationship between the railroads and Hub Group—a hallmark since Phil started the company in 1971—will continue to thrive. Hardin commented:

> *We work really hard at our railroad relationships. We really work hard at delivering what they want from a volume and profit standpoint. If you don't have a seat at the table today, you'll never buy one in the future, and you will get closed out of using intermodal.*[1]

of Schmidt's potential clients had long abandoned the idea of using intermodal shipping transportation.[27]

But, thankfully, that pervasive, negative perception of intermodal was about to change. Hub's Golden Gate operation and all the other hubs would receive an enormous boost the same month that Schmidt arrived in San Francisco. On October 14, 1980, President Jimmy Carter signed the Staggers Rail Act, which would forever change the face of the intermodal industry—with Hub again at the forefront.[28]

### Deregulation Frees the Shipper Agents at Last

As a career congressman from 1949 to 1981, Harley Orrin Staggers was nearing the end of his service in the House of Representatives. One of his chief responsibilities involved serving as the Chairman of the House Committee on Interstate and Foreign Commerce, a position he had held since his election to the post in 1966. By 1980, the railroad industry experienced tremendous pressure from all sides to reform. Economic regulations imposed by the ICC prevented the railroads from offering any flexibility in pricing.[29]

Regulation further prohibited rail carriers from changing their systems or abandoning their outmoded and little-used lines. As a result, the railroads were unable to reign in their costs. The industry experienced financial setbacks because of a regulatory time lag in rate adjustments, a low return on investment, and an inability to raise additional capital. More than 20 percent of the railroads had gone into bankruptcy over the previous decade, and the entire industry experienced a steadily declining market share.[30]

The Staggers Rail Act would free the railroads from these punitive regulations. According to the committee that wrote it, the act was designed "to reform the economic regulation of railroads, to improve the quality of rail service in the United States through financial assistance which encourages railroad restructuring, and for other purposes."[31] The bill quickly passed through Congress and arrived on President Carter's desk. With a stroke of his pen, Carter deregulated the railroad industry, releasing the strictures in place since the Interstate Commerce Act of 1887. At long last, railroads were permitted to determine where they ran trains and how much to charge. The law would help restore the rail industry to financial health, and through a new free-market environment, allow it to prosper as a mighty force in the transportation industry. Stifling federal regulation would be replaced with vigorous market competition.[32]

For shipper agents, deregulation meant they could offer comprehensive services to their customers. Prior to deregulation, Hub and other shipper agents could only provide ramp-to-ramp service. Phil explained:

*With deregulation, intermodalism really blossomed. We could provide complete door-to-door service. It also gave us an opportunity to expand— to create companies in other areas that could perform similar services.[33]*

### The Hub Network Soars Higher

Once deregulation took effect, the railroads acted quickly to survive as an industry. They merged, sought bankruptcy protection, cut off branch lines, and removed disintegrating track. In 1975, there were 75 class I railroads; by 2005, there would be only six.[34] Ironically, as the railroads struggled, Hub continued to grow at an astonishing rate. By April 1982, Hub opened additional operations in New Orleans, Atlanta, and Cleveland.[35]

Training the young executives fell to Hardin, who ran Hub Chicago. Hardin said, "They'd come to Chicago for a week, maybe a little longer. They'd actually stay at my house and bring the wife. They would come to my office and sit right next to me for a week. I had kind of a course put together of how we do what we do, starting from pricing and moving through operations. I could always tell, through the course of that week, whether the guy was going to make it or not. While the husband would sit with me, the wife would sit with the accounting folks and learn how to do the books. A week of that and off they'd go."

Phil and his team always valued independence in these new recruits, but instilled certain limits to prevent too much competition among the hubs. Hardin

recalled, "We tried to define territories. We would say, 'This is your territory, and you can't go outside this territory.' They obeyed those rules pretty much, but these are very aggressive guys, and they're out to make money, and that's what it was all about. They were independent, and they fiercely defended that."[36]

Jim Klingberg, who joined Hub in 1981 as the assistant manager of operations for Hub Milwaukee, recalled the excitement of this entrepreneurial spirit that pervaded throughout Hub's divisions. He said:

*Intermodal was in its early days, at that time, and we were able to literally pick up the phone and call a rates and pricing person at any given railroad. We had all kinds of rail options at that time. Our options were almost limitless, as far as when a customer would call us and ask us for options on pricing and transit times. It was a fun time, very spontaneous, and never a dull moment. The phone rang off the hook because that was before e-mail. You'd be on the phone, and two phones were ringing. You'd have to put someone on hold, and it went on like that all day long. It was just constantly fast-paced. Oftentimes, you'd have the deal done before you hung up the phone. You knew that you had the load. You knew how much money you were making on it, and you knew what the customer needed. The only thing you had to get the customer was the rate, which in some cases, required that you literally type up a rate letter and mail it to them, because there was no such thing as a fax machine or e-mail.[37]*

### A Business Disappointment

Phil frequently visited each of the hubs to check on business. "Each principal had a different level of intensity. If they were honest and lived, ate, and breathed the company, they were successful," he said. Unfortunately, these independent principals did not always share Phil's rigorous personal standards and emphasis on loyalty. "Our confidence, by and large, was rewarded. We did have a few very unfortunate incidences. That was sad, because you don't expect anyone to abuse the authority you've given them," he said.[38]

One of Phil's biggest disappointments involved the first Hub Operating Company based in Detroit. The young man who started the company was

# THE MAKING OF A HUB

PHIL YEAGER HAD A VISION FOR HOW to grow his company. He planned to open up Hub Operating Companies in different parts of the country by enlisting young entrepreneurs, many with railroad experience, to invest in Hub and then serve as the principal or president of the Hub Operating Company.

Phil strongly believed in the husband-and-wife team business concept and encouraged the new owners to involve their wives in running the business. In most cases, the principal and his wife had little or no business experience. Phil explained, "Business experience is something we could not teach them. They had to learn on the job with a little help from Chicago. Each hub was given as much guidance as possible from Tom Hardin and me, and we encouraged them to call for assistance. However, in the end, they had to make the business decisions themselves." Phil and Hardin routinely offered new principals this advice:

- Watch your cash flow, and do not borrow money. All customers should pay within 30 days. If they don't pay, no longer work with them.
- Keep up with your work no matter how many extra hours it takes you because you have to keep up with the movement of freight or your client will suffer (and you will lose him).
- Do not hire extra people until your profits exceed your current costs.
- While on the road making sales calls, stay in contact with your office so you can assist your wife with transportation problems.
- Get to know your vendors and treat them just as well as you treat your customers. You need both of them to have a successful business.
- Build your business. Start with smaller accounts and build your local reputation for customer service.
- Watch your costs. Don't spend a dollar when you only need to spend 50 cents.
- Work hard, work hard, work hard.[1]

extremely successful, and the business grew quickly. However after eight years of success, he abruptly left Hub to work independently, taking the majority of Hub Detroit employees and accounts with him. Eventually, he lured away three principals and many employees from the New Orleans, Memphis, and Toledo hubs.[39]

Joe Wallace, an entry-level operations employee at Hub City Detroit at the time, recalled the immediate impact the split had on Hub. "It really rocked the company and had a significant impact on Detroit, Memphis, New Orleans, and Toledo. There were rumors within the industry that Hub was going out of business and closing the doors. So there was, I think, fear from a customer and vendor standpoint that Hub wouldn't be around, and this drove business away from Hub by design. A rumor like that is devastating. In fact, I think their strategy was to spread the rumors until eventually, they hoped, Hub would run out of cash and have to close."[40]

Upon learning of the upheaval, Phil and Joyce immediately rushed to Detroit to establish new operations. Wallace and Gene Corinescu first met them during this troubling time. Wallace recalled:

*I worked directly under the former Detroit manager. When Phil arrived, I liked him immediately and recognized that he was a man I could relate to and work for. The structure of the office was there, but there was no business. It was very difficult, but we fought back and slowly rebuilt the office. We said to customers, "We want your business. We earned it once before, and we're going to earn it again." To the surprise of everyone, we had staying power, and we slowly dismantled their plan to drive Hub from the Detroit marketplace.*[41]

About this disquieting episode, Phil said, "I thought of this person as a son, and he really let me down. It was a terrible disappointment when he left, but one that taught us many lessons."[42]

### The Los Angeles Connection

Determined to crack the tough Los Angeles market, Phil brought in Jim Decker in 1983—who had a great deal of experience working for the railroad in intermodal—to see if he could break into this very difficult market. "When Phil offered me the position, I talked it over with my wife, and we decided it was a great opportunity," Decker recalled.

At the time, the business consisted of one account. "And they handed me that one account from Chicago. It produced maybe 20 to 30 trailers a month, and that was it," Decker said. "It took us a while to get up and running. We planned to open in July, but there was a phone strike that lasted a month. Once the strike was settled, we really went for it. But I probably worked for three months before I got my own accounts."[43]

Decker recounted the make-or-break mentality of this business:

*I was scared to death. It was just my wife, Nancy, and I, and we had taken all the money we had saved to get into this business. We had invested with a 25-percent ownership of Hub Los Angeles. My wife and I had saved about $30,000. It was $25,000 for our 25 percent of the company. So now we're down to $5,000. What am I going to do with three little kids? I was 41 years old. I had to make this thing work. If it didn't work, we'd be out on the street. I was pushing myself through being scared. But we lost money that first year—something like $40,000. We had a lot of expenses that year. We just weren't doing that much business.*

Things improved from then on. Decker said, "We made $10,000 in the second year. Then, in the third year, we made $100,000. And it just went up from there. Then, as a company, our business grew from two people, to three, to seven, and right on up. It was just amazing. But those first two years were shaky."[44]

### A Time for Celebration

Hub continued its upward spiral by opening companies throughout the country during the early 1980s. The network of hubs expanded to include Portland, Kansas, Tennessee, Minnesota, and Los Angeles by September 1983.[45]

Phil and Joyce decided to host a celebration in recognition of Hub's growing business family. They instituted an annual three-day event in Longboat Key, Florida, bringing together all the principals and their families from the company's Subchapter S corporations. "It was as much a celebration as a business gathering. It wasn't just for the guys but for the women, too," Phil said. "It was very helpful that the wives were so involved. They worked as hard as their husbands. These gals were tremendously important to the overall success of the company."

Besides meeting with the principals as a group to discuss business, the Yeagers hosted a dinner party at a local restaurant for the families to enjoy some camaraderie and good food. The annual gathering provided a venue for all the principals to discuss successes, troubleshoot problems, and develop personal relationships with Hub associates and their families, who otherwise worked independently while scattered across the country.[46]

Shortly after the first annual gathering, David left Hub St. Louis and went back to Chicago with his wife to take over the sales department there. "Although Chicago was growing, the sales group needed to improve," said David. We were making very small fees and had hardly any customers of our own. So the first thing I did was start to turn up the heat on all of the salespeople. I think they were all gone within a year. With new salespeople in place, we grew in volume and profitability."[47]

### Double-Stack Car Debuts

Because of the deregulation in the railroad industry, Hub required a top-notch sales staff at every site to take advantage of the new opportunities that presented themselves. Besides deregulation, American President Lines' introduction of the double-stack car or stack train in 1984 enlivened the railroad industry, greatly enhancing intermodal business. This innovation enabled trains to double their capacity by stacking containers two-high. David explained:

*The commercialization of the stack train is a pivotal point in the history of intermodal. It really created the rail economics that we experience today and has made the rails much more compet-*

*itive. The double-stack is about 40 percent more efficient than the flatcar, and that means the savings could be passed on to customers, while creating a lot more profitability and business for the railroads and for us.[48]*

Phil concurred, "The rails could finally make money in intermodal, and the double-stack container has been a very important part of their overall financial success ever since. It revolutionized our industry."[49]

It also poised Hub, once again, for unprecedented growth.

# The Innovative Double-Stack

IN 1977, SOUTHERN PACIFIC Railroad test-marketed the first double-stack car for container traffic.[1] These cars (also called well cars) resemble flatcars but have a container-size depression, or well, in the middle of the car. This depression allows for sufficient clearance to load two containers on top of each other in a "double-stack" arrangement.[2] In traditional rail shipments, a frame-and-wheel chassis was loaded onto the flatcar, which held a single container for shipment.[3]

Despite the double-stack's advantages, including increased load capacity—which leads to larger shipments and ultimately increased profits for the railroad—the rest of the industry was slow to embrace it. But when American President Lines (APL), in 1984, boldly developed a network of double-stack trains that could crisscross the United States, the industry recognized the financial benefits, overcame its initial hesitation, and quickly adopted the innovation.[4]

APL's double-stack car almost doubled train capacity because two containers could be stacked on top of each other. Each double-stack car carried up to 10 containers on a length of

train that, in the past, handled only six. Further, the removal of both the trailer's frame and wheels from the container greatly reduced the weight, thus allowing for more freight per train.[5]

Besides carrying more freight, the double-stack helped reduce freight damage because of its improved stability, resulting from the removal of the wheels and chassis. This benefit alone helped convince previously skeptical shippers to ship using the double-stack containers. In the past, shippers sustained heavy damage to their freight from swaying and strong vibrations created by the long distance between the wheels on traditional flatcars.[6]

The introduction of the double-stack car served as an important milestone in the evolution and heightened success of the intermodal industry. "It was a huge development for our industry," Phil Yeager said.[7]

An example of the double-stack container introduced nationally in 1984. This significant advancement paved the way for substantial growth in the intermodal industry.

When Hub introduced this logo in 1989, it had diversified and expanded to include a total of 23 separate divisions.

# CHAPTER FOUR

# UNPRECEDENTED GROWTH

## 1985–1991

*By the mid-1980s, we had established a real trust with not only the shippers but with the railroads and drayage companies. It took 15 years to gain their trust.*

—Phillip Yeager

IN THE MID-1980s, HUB CONTINued to experience astounding growth. Much of its expansion could be attributed to three main factors. First, the Staggers Rail Act of 1980 allowed Hub to offer customers better rates and a wider variety of services. Second, the introduction of the double-stack car increased train capacity by as much as 40 percent.[1] And third, the ever-increasing network of Hub satellite offices, each strategically located in freight transportation centers, helped solidify Hub's growing presence in the intermodal industry.[2]

"Much of our success resulted from being the only logistics provider with a real operating network," Phillip Yeager said. "The major shippers, who are a very large part of our business, want representation in these places, because they have multiple plants and multiple distribution areas. Our people are there and can help them solve their problems."[3]

But with the expansion of the facilities came inevitable growing pains. Reaching consensus from the various Hub Operating Companies proved extremely challenging (there would be 22 separate offices by September 1985).[4] David Yeager recalled, "It was very difficult, very complex to build consensus. You basically had to achieve consensus by making decisions that

would benefit each corporation economically. You try to keep them in tow by holding annual board meetings and by just trying to make sure that they were on the right track. But for the most part, they had complete autonomy, which created a very difficult management challenge."[5]

Determined to keep the explosive growth on track, despite the management challenges, Phil decided to reach out to Fortune 500 companies that could provide Hub with the national client base he sought.

In order to gain the attention of the larger companies, Phil believed the perception of Hub required a change. "All our Hub Operating Companies needed to come across to our shippers as a single, unified company," Phil said.[6]

### The Creation of Hub Group

To transform the perception of Hub, Phil decided to establish a new business entity that would serve as an umbrella organization for the

---

In 1991, the Intermodal Transportation Association bestowed its highest honor on Phil Yeager by naming him its "Man of the Year" for his outstanding contributions to the intermodal industry.

numerous Hub Operating Companies. Tom Hardin recalled the background circumstances that led to the creation of the new organization, "All the Hub Operating Companies came to us for leadership, and, at the same time, we're trying to run Hub Chicago. So, that's when Phil came up with a plan. He said, 'I think we need to have somebody else run Hub Chicago. You and I should form a new entity so we can have better control over all the hubs.' That's when we formed Hub Group—in October 1985."

Hardin recalled how they chose the name Hub Group for the new oversight company, "The name itself has kind of a funny origin. We were kicking around what we should call it. We've got all these Hub Cities and I said, 'You know what? I just saw a magazine ad about Chubb. That's kind of a funny name. We're Hub and they're Chubb—the Chubb Group of companies. How about Hub Group? That makes sense.' So Hub was really, I think, based on Chubb."[7]

With a chosen name, the Hub Group became a reality, and the leadership team was put in place. Phil took the helm as chairman, and Hardin became president. In turn, David was appointed as president of Hub Chicago. Dan Hardman, who previously served as sales manager for Hub Chicago, moved into the position of vice president under David.

The creation of the Hub Group provided necessary oversight responsibilities for the various Hub offices. Hardin explained, "All the hubs needed group insurance, master contracts for all of the vendors—just a whole myriad of things were required. We needed to be able to fight their battles for them at a high level with the railroads. Each hub was viewed as just a local Milwaukee or Atlanta or Kansas company, but we could harness the strength of this whole organization with the Hub Group. We created financial requirements, financial statements—all of those things." In order to manage the financial aspects of the business, Hub Group brought in a comptroller, who reported to Phil and kept a close watch on the financial activities for each of the hubs.[8]

One of Hub Group's main missions involved taking the collective bargaining power of the individual hubs to buy insurance, make rail contacts, and secure business from Fortune 500 compa-

Dan Hardman, left,
one-time sales manager for Hub Chicago, became its vice president in 1985 when Hub incorporated. Hardman, pictured here chatting with David Wenger, president of Eastern America Trucking, went on to become president of Hub Chicago and later executive vice president of intermodal operations for Hub Group.

nies. Tom Reisinger, who opened Hub Indianapolis in 1987, explained, "The company culture was one of, 'This is my business. I'm here to make money. Hub has given me a great opportunity with its relationships with the railroads and its national stature to grow my business.' There was a great esprit de corps between the different offices. Yes, certain offices would compete with each other, but we also had to work well with each other."[9]

With the intensified power the new organization brought to the table, Phil could now aggressively pursue larger customers, including Fortune 500 companies, that would elevate Hub to a higher level. He felt so strongly about the importance of moving in this new direction that he created a new division for the Hub Group called the National Accounts Program.[10]

### The National Accounts Program Debuts

"Even after deregulation occurred in 1980, I recognized that the large Fortune 500 companies in this country were not using intermodal. They didn't like it because it wasn't a complete service. We had a very small sales force, and we didn't get out there and sell complete service as quickly as we could have, and we didn't get the other hubs to sell it on a regular basis. National accounts are very different than just selling to an individual plant or small company. Selling to national accounts involves working with people in other territories. It really requires a much higher-skilled sales individual, and they're very expensive," Phil explained.[11]

The Hub Group, Phil determined, needed to learn how to deal with Fortune 500 corporations. "These large companies had very heavy requirements, a lot more than smaller firms, so they needed someone who really could come in and devote time to working with them," he said.[12] The National Accounts Program would also be useful in helping change perceptions. "Because of their structures, these Fortune 500 companies were difficult to call on," Phil explained. "At that time, major corporations had shifted control of transportation decisions from traffic departments to logistics people. That required some adjustment and some missionary work. Many of our customers had been taught that trucking was the only way to go. Many people felt that intermodal was an inferior product and had to be sold at a discount. The fact is, it is just as good as truck or even better in some lanes."

To set up and run the National Accounts Program, Hub hired John Donnell, who had extensive railroad experience through 20 years with the Illinois Central Gulf railroad. Donnell brought in other executives, each hired to target a select group of large national accounts. From its inception, the program proved a stellar success. Within five years, the National Accounts Program would account for 35 percent of Hub's overall business.[13]

Donnell attributes much of the program's success to Phil's leadership example. He said:

*What set us apart from the beginning was the quality of the people, and the quality of our leadership. Phil Yeager was like a second father to me. You just truly went to bat every day knowing that you must succeed to please him. I think he hired the kind of people that did that. They would put forth every effort, but unlike many of our competi-*

*tors, he had a set of standards that involved honesty and integrity that I think the others didn't have. We had people that were above reproach in terms of doing the right thing. If somebody tried to get them to do something that would produce benefit to the customer at even the railroad's expense, they would literally not do it because they knew they had to live with themselves. Every deed creates a ripple effect. We hired really outstanding people that could have been successful in any selling venture.*[14]

Relating an anecdote that illustrates Phil's leadership, Donnell explained: "Phil reminds me of the Debbie Fields' example about cookies. When one of the managers at a store was trying to sell 8-hour-old cookies instead of 3-hour-old ones, he said to Fields, 'They're still good enough.' She replied, 'Good enough never is.' I think that was the way we lived our lives. Being good enough was not with enough distinction that you would get remembered. When our people interviewed customers, they really wanted to understand the problem, and the problem behind the problems, and then solve those problems. We understood our customers' needs and our ability

The creation of Hub Group in October 1985 proved a historic event for the company. Phil took the helm as chairman, while David became president of Hub Chicago. Tom Hardin (not pictured) became president of Hub Group.

After launching his career at Hub's Detroit office, Joe Wallace moved to Toledo in 1987 to run Hub Ohio.

to deliver solutions by entwining all of the players, the railroads, the equipment owners, and the customers' facilities."[15]

**Hub Cities Proliferate**

As the National Accounts Program took off, Hub continued its expansion of Hub Operating Companies across the United States. A Houston office opened in September 1985, Florida in March 1986, Alabama in August, and New York state that same year.[16] As in previous operations, Hub pursued highly ethical young executives eager for an ownership stake, who were not afraid of hard work.

Looking for principals who live within close proximity to the desired business proved an important consideration as well, recalled Tom Reisinger. "I'd worked for John Donnell for six years at the Illinois Central Gulf Railroad until they downsized, and I took a severance package. So there I am calling from the basement of my father-in-law's house in Dayton trying to find a job. John put me in touch with Phil who offered

me Baltimore, the Mid-Atlantic office. But a week after they started to talk to me about it, they found a person from CSX who lived there. So they said, 'Hang in there. We like you.' The next opportunity was Philadelphia. This time they found someone from Conrail who lived there. Again, they said to hang in there. This was in August, and finally at the end of September, they decided to carve up a couple of territories that were basically dead zones for the offices that controlled those territories at that time. That's how I ended up with Indianapolis and part of Kentucky."

In typical Hub fashion, Reisinger and his wife, Margo, became president and vice president, respectively, and the two worked to establish the office in that territory. "I had never sold in that marketplace, nor did I know anybody, but what I did know is that I owned a percentage of the profits of the company. I knew it was a chance for me at age 37 to have a stake."[17]

Joe Wallace, who began his career with Hub's Detroit office and became president of Hub Ohio in Toledo in 1987, remembered the importance the Hub Group's management had on his and the other divisions:

*It is doubtful that the dynamics created as a result of the personalities of all the principals could ever be duplicated. Different backgrounds, unique personalities, each one made contributions to the organization as a whole. This was a good group of people, all very bright and talented. This was a tribute to Phil because he assembled us.*

*Sales calls with Phil were always fun. He loved to visit with customers and was always able to relate to them and knew many of their employees nationwide. I know Hub Ohio employees loved and looked forward to his visits to our office. Always at the end of the year I would tell Phil, "Wow, we had a great year. I don't think I'll be able to top it." He would laugh and simply say, "Sure you will Joe—you'll see!" And he was always right. We had another important goal: Keep Phil happy. We did that by working hard, staying out of trouble, and delivering good quarterly and annual reports.*[18]

Obviously, the original formula for success that Phil and Joyce created continued to generate winning operations. By 1989, the Hub network had grown to include 23 subsidiaries.[19]

Back in 1971, Don Maltby, Sr., a Nabisco transportation executive, took a risk and convinced his bosses to give the nascent Hub City Terminal, Inc., a try at solving Nabisco's transportation problems. Maltby's faith in Hub forged a 30-plus-year successful business relationship with Hub and Nabisco, which continues even today.[42] In July 1990, Phil heard about Don Maltby's son, Don Maltby, Jr., and sought to hire him. Don first went with the N&W Railroad, then Sherwin Williams in Cleveland, finally joining Hub in 1990.[20]

Maltby, Jr., recalled the circumstances that led to his good fortune. "My career was with Sherwin Williams at the time. I ran their transportation operations and was living in Cleveland. We reached out to Hub to see if they were interested in providing intermodal opportunities. I was told that there were some issues with the Cleveland division at the time, and that I should call the corporate office. So I picked up the phone and called Phil Yeager to introduce myself. I found out that their Cleveland hub president had embezzled a large sum of money. He'd basically bankrupted the company. Well, long story short, I'd always wanted to own my own business. I said, 'To me, it sounds like something that just needs an infusion of marketing and sales and some operational discipline.'"[21]

Phil offered to show Maltby, Jr., the financials, and the two quickly struck up a deal. In the next eight years, Maltby, Jr., saw a $4 million-a-year franchise with three employees grow to an $89 million-a-year business with 37 people. Maltby, Jr., said:

*We needed to instill in our people and our customers the winning attitude that Phil had built with the rest of Hub. Hub is a tremendous company with tremendous pride. That made a huge difference and was a direct component of our success.*[22]

Mike Blackwell, a longtime Hub customer in the forest products industry, recalled:

*One of the things that Hub offered was Phil himself. I mean Phil is, to me, just a true gentleman in the industry and very knowledgeable,*

Both Don Maltby, Sr., and Jr., have long histories with Hub Group. As a Nabisco executive, Don Maltby, Sr., initiated a lasting relationship with Hub that started in 1971. Don Maltby, Jr., took over Hub Cleveland in 1990 and successfully grew the business there.

*committed to quality and service, and he certainly has a good reputation. He pioneered intermodal and made the service seamless. It has to be just like shipping it on a truck. That's really part of the service Phil came into the industry with. It was putting all those pieces together.*

*Typically, industrial transportation departments don't have the staff to contact the ramps, contact the drayage companies, negotiate with the railroads, lease or purchase equipment, all those types of things. Phil pulled that all together. So, the service he provided to us was what was so appealing.*[23]

### Diversification of Services

Hub aggressively sought to anticipate shippers' needs and implement solutions to satisfy them. With the creation of Hub Highway Services in 1989, Phil would satisfy the shippers' desire for comprehensive services, which would include trucking transportation. Phil recalled, "Going into the truck brokerage business was a very important step, because customers were asking, 'Why

can you give us intermodal service, but you can't give us truck service?'" The new division created an over-the-road extension of the company's traditional transportation services, and it also established another profit center for the company. "We also diversified because we were 100 percent intermodal prior to this time," Phil explained.[24]

In the first six months of operation, Hub Highway Services garnered 4,363 trailer loads with revenues of $3.5 million. By 1990, after the first full year of operation, the trucking operation handled 22,000 trailer loads and generated more than $17 million in sales.[25] But the profitable launch of Hub Highway Services was nearly overshadowed by a development that shook up the entire intermodal industry.[26]

### The Competition Ramps Up

Rumors of trucking giant J. B. Hunt's intention to enter and compete in the intermodal market emerged during the annual Intermodal Association of North America (IANA) meeting in 1989. The eventual confirmation of the news threw the entire industry into a state of shock. Everyone, that is, but Phil and Hub. "People went around saying, 'Well, I'm closing up the business.' People in our industry just panicked. There were a lot of surprised people, and some very scared people, but I said, 'We're going to do one thing. We're going to get better. We're not ducking anybody. We'll compete with anybody.'"[27]

Phil's resolve proved as good as his word. By the time Hunt and Santa Fe Railroad announced their joint service agreement in mid-December 1989, Hub was finalizing plans for its own high-speed, line-haul business. In January 1990, Hub introduced its Bantam Premium Intermodal Service between Chicago and Los Angeles. Hardin

explained, "While it was a high-speed service, I think the really important feature was that it provided an on-time guarantee to our customers. We would actually have to pay a significant penalty if we were late. We moved thousands of loads, and I think we only paid one or two penalties throughout the whole process."[28]

The service was so successful that by September of that year, it had expanded to seven major transportation corridors. By February 1991, the Bantam Premium Intermodal Service mushroomed across the United States, this time to include 74 intermodal corridors—daily.[29]

Nabisco, Kellogg, and Spiegel, along with several automobile companies were among the businesses that took advantage of this high-speed service. Phil commented:

*A lot of people predicted that the intermodal marketing companies were on their way out and would be gone within a five-year period. It was a time when our industry could have collapsed. It did the opposite for us; it stimulated us. J. B. Hunt provided us with real tough competition, and it spurred us on. We changed the way we operated our company dramatically in the next few years. We knew we had to diversify and expand our services, or the negative predictions would come true.[30]*

Mark Yeager, Phil's son and Hub Group's current president and chief operating officer, concurred, "When Hunt and other trucking companies entered the field, they gave us the hardest time. We were accustomed to competing with mom-and-pop intermodal marketing companies that were very decentralized. Then, suddenly, we're up against these sophisticated, asset-based companies that really understand the value of

# WHAT IS DRAYAGE?

INTERMODAL IS AN INDUSTRY WITH A language all its own. Consider the term *intermodal drayage*. Few people outside the industry of transportation know what the term means despite the fact that intermodal drayage is a multibillion dollar industry employing thousands of people. An old English word, drayage refers to the haulage of goods using a dray or vehicle without wheels. In the context of intermodalism, drayage refers to the local pickup and delivery services performed by trucking companies as part of the intermodal process.

In a typical drayage transaction, a local truck driver, called a drayman, picks up an empty container and transports it to a shipper for loading.

Goods are transferred to the container at the shipper's facility. From there, the drayman drives the loaded container to a rail terminal where it is loaded on a train headed to a rail ramp proximate to the container's ultimate destination. After the train arrives at the destination rail ramp, the delivery drayman is notified of the container's arrival. The delivery drayman picks up the load at the terminal and transports it to the receiver who accepts the load and unloads the goods, thereby making the container available for its next load and move.[1]

Drayage companies come in all shapes and sizes, ranging from a single tractor owner-operator to large, sophisticated, multimillion-dollar operations performing services throughout the country.

getting velocity and balance out of your equipment, and understand how to manage everything. They have people with advanced degrees working complex mathematical algorithms to help them with pricing questions. These were competitors we weren't ready to deal with. But, we certainly figured out very quickly how to do it."[31]

One upside to J. B. Hunt's entrance into the intermodal market involved an acknowledgment, at long last, from the railroads and freight customers that intermodal often offered the most cost-effective way to ship goods. Just two years prior to signing the agreement with Santa Fe Railroad, Hunt vehemently asserted it would never enter the intermodal business. When Gilbert E. Carmichael, federal railroad adminis-

trator at the time, learned of the Hunt-Santa Fe agreement, he said, "If intermodal service is good enough for J. B. Hunt, the industry must be doing a lot of things right. Shippers and logistics managers considering service options really need to reevaluate their thinking about intermodal service. It's obvious J. B. Hunt has."[32]

Hub Group's James Gaw, current executive vice president of sales, concurred, "Hunt had a

Opposite: After introducing Bantam Premium Intermodal Service between Chicago and Los Angeles in 1990, Hub quickly expanded this hugely successful high-speed, line-haul business across the United States.

Right: A joyous event in the Yeager family—Debra and brother David Yeager, and Mark with his new wife Heather on their wedding day in 1990.

With the institution of the Quality Drayage Program in 1990, Hub Group focused on quality control for its drayage partners. The Quality Drayage Program governed the way in which drayage companies performed services for Hub.

Participants in the program committed to providing high-quality service along with clean and safe equipment, while maintaining a defined on-time performance level. They also agreed to follow specified procedures designed to minimize freight loss and damage. In return, these companies became Hub's primary drayage partners.[35]

### Raising the Bar on Customer Service

In order to provide even greater customer service to its client base, Hub created two more service areas before the end of 1990, Hub Group Distribution Services and its Logistics Division now called Unyson Logistics. Hub Group Distribution Services specialized in customized, single-source consolidation and door-to-door distribution of multiple shipments.[36]

Current Executive Vice President of Logistics, Don Maltby, Jr., explained the purpose of his division, "We define logistics as transportation man-

great name as a motor carrier. Intermodal had always been kind of a stepchild from the standpoint of how people looked at it as a service versus highway. Hunt really legitimized intermodal in a lot of people's eyes. It improved the perception of the product."[33] Hub had already pushed the Highway Services Division into high gear when Hunt entered the market, and Hub's early success with Bantam Premium Intermodal Service helped secure Hub's hold on its share of the intermodal business. Tom Holzmann, president of Hub Rio Grande Terminals, commented, "The creation of Hub Highway Services allowed us to be more than a single-mode carrier. It allowed us to compete with our staunchest competitors—the long-haul truckers. This was a significant development for Hub."[34]

Above and right: Hub enters the computer age with the introduction of its Electronic Data Interchange (EDI) system housed in Hub's first "computer room" in 1990.

agement and bimodal expertise. We offer technology as a solution and resources to provide the solution."[37] To further expand on the subject, Phil commented, "We realized as the 1990s began that logistics was becoming more and more important. We decided that we had to get ready for this. I felt from the beginning that Hub had a place in this logistics market. Again, it's part of taking care of our customers' needs."[38]

### Business Enhancements

As the final decade of the 20th century began, Hub aggressively worked to establish itself as a united company, created new divisions to satisfy and exceed client demands, and competed successfully when new players like J. B. Hunt entered the intermodal industry. The always-forward-thinking Phil Yeager initiated two more key advancements to help secure the future prosperity and success of his company. Hub opened its first international office—in Canada—in 1991.

Then, to stay on the cutting edge and deliver customers even faster service, Hub introduced its Electronic Data Interchange (EDI) system. This system provided real-time monitoring of all of Hub's shipments. This enhancement would increase efficiency and improve customer service, important priorities for the company.[39]

Capping off the stunning 20-year growth of the company, Phil earned an outstanding business honor when he was named "Man of the Year" by the Intermodal Transportation Association. In his typical modest fashion, Phil said:

*It was an honor to be given this recognition by my peers. The honor wasn't given to me—it was given to our entire company.*[40]

Hub continued to surpass the dreams of Phil Yeager, a self-described "hard-headed German," to unparalleled achievement. But personal challenges and business hardships lie on the road just up ahead.

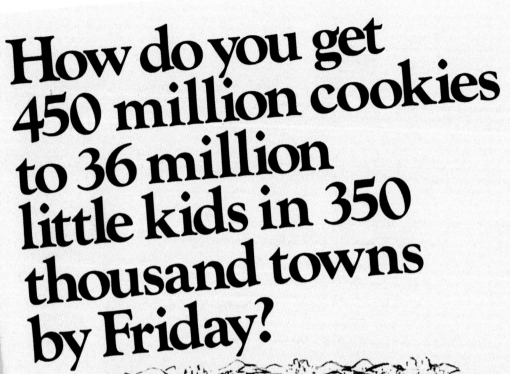

# How do you get 450 million cookies to 36 million little kids in 350 thousand towns by Friday?

Little kids count on Oreo® cookies.

And Oreo® cookies count on Hub City Terminals to get them there on time, all the time.

That's what the Hub Concept is all about in serving shippers. From first trailer loading to final delivery, we handle total shipping assignments via the best carriers, with the fastest and finest service, and the lowest rates. That's the kind of total service package at the best bottom line that we've become known for providing.

It's why Nabisco Brands counts on us. And so can you.

## The Hub Group, Inc.

A member of IMA (Intermodal Marketing Association) • 1035 Havens Court, Downers Grove, IL 60615  312-971-2277

By the early 1990s, Hub's enduring relationship with Nabisco passed the 20-year mark. This advertisement touts the importance of fast and reliable service, and Hub's ability to deliver it consistently.

# CHAPTER FIVE

# PROSPERITY DESPITE CHALLENGES

## 1992–1995

*It's a tough business. Five dollars a load makes all the difference in the world.*

—Tom Hardin

HUB'S DAZZLING NEW ARRAY of service divisions, created at the start of the 1990s, helped the company to keep pace in the fiercely competitive world of intermodal. Its long-term close relationships with the railroads and its reputation for unparalleled customer service further enhanced its position in the industry. In addition, many of the all-important Fortune 500 companies, along with other current and potential customers, began viewing the various Hub Cities as a large, single company. Soon, the company would unify in a much more formal way by going public. In doing so, Hub would further increase its momentum toward even greater heights as a key logistics provider.[1]

Hub customers and its business partners would consistently point to Phillip Yeager's example of integrity, strong work ethic, and passion for customer service as among the secrets to his company's growth and success. As his son David's role in the company increased, this second-generation Yeager shared his father's noble principles and his stellar reputation within and outside of Hub.

While working full-time at Hub, David attended the Graduate School of Business at the prestigious University of Chicago part-time until he earned his MBA in 1987. "I had a degree in chemistry. Except when it came to transporting toxic chemicals, there weren't really many applications for my degree in our business," David said. "The MBA really just formalized all the knowledge I had acquired through my experiences."[2] According to Phil:

*David's greatest assistance to Tom and me was his tremendous knowledge of the large Hub Chicago office operations and his closeness with all the hub principals. They knew him and liked him, and they spoke to him about a lot of things that they wouldn't have brought up to Tom or me. I had conservative ideas about the company and didn't like to take chances. Tom was almost as conservative as I was. But he also had the confidence of all the hubs. They all talked to him, and he was a good listener. David was now a mature man, and we needed three heads instead of two.[3]*

In recognition of David's increased involvement in the company, he became vice-chairman of Hub Group in January 1992.[4] "David has worked his way from the ground up and has done a great job," Phil commented about his son. "He has brought a lot of great ideas and zip to the company."[5]

---

Tom Hardin, Hub's first employee and closest associate to the Yeagers, was named chief operating officer and director of Hub Group in March 1995.

Equally as proud of her eldest son's record with the company, Joyce, who remained a vice president at Hub, hoped their youngest son, Mark, would join the company fold as well.[6] Mark, who was 12 years younger than David, had decided to study law. "I sort of led him in the direction of law. He went to Georgetown Law School and did very well," Phil commented. "He got a job with a big firm in downtown Chicago, but I was always hoping that he would come work at Hub."[7] Mark graduated in 1989 and practiced anti-trust and securities litigation for about three years before heeding the call to join Hub.[6]

### Another Yeager on Board

In May 1992, Mark transitioned from the practice of law to join Hub as a full-time employee. "I always knew that I'd want to come back to the company at some point, but I also wanted to do my own thing for a little bit of time," he said. "But you know, three years was plenty of time in the legal business to make me want to come back."[7]

Part of Mark's impetus for joining Hub came at the urging of his mother, Joyce. Following a diagnosis of cancer in September 1991, Joyce discussed with Phil her wish for Mark to work in the family business. "She expressed that desire," Phil recalled. "So I immediately asked Mark and he said, 'I'll be there'"[8]

At Hub, one of Mark's first orders of business involved developing Hub's own version of the then-popular management paradigm called Total Quality Management (TQM). At the time, many American businesses utilized this system of management developed by a statistician named W. Edwards Deming in the early 1950s. Not surprisingly, several of Deming's tenets emphasize both purveyor and customer satisfaction—important business concepts that paralleled Phil's own personal business philosophy.[9] Mark recalled:

*The entire shipper community was getting very engaged in TQM. They really wanted to see processes in place with their underlying carriers. A number of companies, particularly those that had Asian ownership, were substantially farther down the path, so we benchmarked with some other companies to understand where we needed to go. Then, in Hub fashion, we went out and began training our folks on TQM.*[10]

When Hub officially incorporated on March 8, 1995, David Yeager became CEO.

With all of Hub's divisions scattered across the United States, Mark found training and implementation of TQM a formidable challenge. "I believe I taught process management 40 times in about a year-and-a-half," he said. "We tried to give everyone a common language as much as anything. We had at that time, 29 different offices and 29 different ways of doing business. We tried to make sure everybody was analyzing the effectiveness of their business in the same way."

Although a difficult feat, Mark provided the necessary tools to the various hub organizations in order to make the TQM system a successful endeavor for Hub. He also handled legal affairs for Hub, which he described as "not very complex until we went public."[11]

When asked to comment on his sons' initiation into the family business, Phil said, "They were both put in jobs where they were learning the business, even though they probably knew more than most of the people in the company because of all the talk about Hub at home. Both of my sons slowly built their reputation with the company based on their hard work."[12]

### A Hub Competitor Shuts Its Doors

A group of U.S. shippers formed the Industrial Trailer on Flatcar Association (ITOFCA) in the 1960s as a not-for-profit organization created to serve the shippers intermodal transportation needs. Tom Hardin explained:

*They were the forerunner and flagship organization designed to serve the intermodal needs of their member shippers. Designed as a not-for-profit cooperative, their charter prohibited them from hiring*

**In August, you made us the largest independent shippers agent in the world. Again.**

**Thank you.**

**The ⊕ Hub Group, Inc.**
1035 Havens Court, Downers Grove, IL 60515
**312-971-2277**
National Accounts Office, Stamford, Conn.: 203-968-0044

*salespeople and providing direct sales and marketing to their members. They could not call on their own customer base from a sales standpoint. They were hamstrung.*[13]

With the Staggers Rail Act of 1980, competition really heated up, and ITOFCA, with all its chartered limitations, quickly discovered that it couldn't effectively compete. As the 1980s progressed, ITOFCA continued to lose business. With the entrance of J. B. Hunt and Schneider Trucking into the already overcrowded intermodal field, ITOFCA saw its customer base dwindle off.

Harry Inda, a previous ITOFCA employee, went to work for Hub in 1987. "I actually left ITOFCA during one of their downsizings in 1987. They had trouble surviving in the environment created by the deregulation—they couldn't keep up."[14]

Finally, in 1993, the association dismantled its operations. "They just closed the doors without any notice," Hardin said. "There were a lot of shipments out there in transit—thousands of them—as a matter of fact. So many of these customers called us and of course we said, 'We will help you out.' And we did. We moved their freight and, in the process, their business came to Hub."

Aside from picking up the majority of the association's clients, Hub also hired several of its executives. "It was an unfortunate situation," Hardin said. "You never want to win by default, but in this case, we were there, and the situation resulted in a lot of new customers for Hub."[15]

### National Media Attention

Hub experienced another major success in 1993. Tom Reisinger, who started Hub City Indianapolis, landed publishing giant R. R. Donnelley & Sons as a client in his fifth year of operation. Reisinger recalled:

*R. R. Donnelley & Sons set up a central dispatch for about 15 of their plants in central Indiana. All of them needed intermodal service which, of course, we set up for them. We did $15 million in sales that year—$9 million of which came from our work for R. R. Donnelley & Sons alone. That's when we really took off. Believe it or not, but, at the time, only my wife, Margo, who also taught school, and I ran the whole operation.*[16]

# THE LEGACY OF JOYCE YEAGER

**P**HILLIP YEAGER ALWAYS SHARED THE credit for the successful business model that would form the basis of the mighty Hub Group with his wife, Joyce. He often described her as a force of nature. "She was cofounder of the company and a tremendous asset. She was very detail-focused, and we worked as equals, although she thought she was in charge," he said. As Hub expanded over the years, Joyce continued to serve as a model for other company employees. "Women always looked up to Joyce," Phil explained.

While Joyce valiantly battled cancer, she continued to work at the office until May 1992, when her illness progressed, and she could no longer fulfill her duties at Hub.

A few months later, at age 63, Joyce passed away on December 26, 1992. "During the days before her death, we talked about so many things we didn't have the opportunity to do previously. Joyce gave me a lot of good advice. Even when she was very ill, she would write me little notes. We actually shared a lot of laughs near the end," said Phil.

From supporting Phil when he left his job with the railroad to pursue his dream, to working tirelessly side by side with Phil, Joyce greatly affected not only the lives of her family but also those of the company that she loved so dearly. Her daughter, Debra Jensen, recalled, "Mom was an extremely hard worker and very smart. She kept the family together; she was so organized. She was the real communicator in the family. She and Dad always set a great example for everyone in the company."

Phil recalled, "Joyce was a loving, caring mom—a tough mom with her kids, and I mean as long as they lived in our home, they obeyed our rules. As a wife, she was terrific. I always thought of her as a beautiful woman, and she was striking. She had a great figure, even at 60. She was athletic, strong-willed, but willing to compromise—occasionally—like all good wives do. She was a good cook who had to have her one night a week out to a nice restaurant."[1]

### The Joyce Yeager Scholarships

Both Joyce and Phil were exercise enthusiasts. "Mom played tennis regularly, and I remember Dad swam laps every night after work," Debra said. Near the end, Phil talked to Joyce about establishing a remembrance for her. Phil recalled:

*One of the things we discussed a few weeks before her death was how she wanted to be remembered. She just laughed, so I said,*

Right: Phil and Joyce share a picture-perfect moment during the holidays in the 1970s.

Left: A charming formal portrait of Phil and Joyce taken in 1992.

Right: The Yeagers gather for a formal occasion in 1989. Joyce enjoyed spending time with her extended family. From left to right: Heather Yeager (Mark's wife), Julia Yeager (David's wife), Mark, Joyce, Phil, Debra, and David.

*"How about a scholarship for a Hub employee's child at the University of Cincinnati?"*

*She really didn't reply, but I knew she liked the idea because she wasn't able to attend college, as her parents couldn't afford it. She had a little inferiority complex about this, particularly when she joined various clubs whose memberships were pretty much comprised of college grads. This didn't keep her from becoming president of three of these clubs, and invariably being asked to be a model in their fashion shows.*

*She also felt she couldn't speak before a group of people, but on numerous occasions, she had to run the meeting and give speeches, and she turned out to be a very good speaker who always used humor to make her point.*

After Joyce's untimely passing, Phil set up the scholarship that he and Joyce had discussed. He added another scholarship in 2001.

### The Joyce E. Yeager Hub Group Scholarship

Established by Phil to honor his deceased wife, this scholarship provides a $10,000 scholarship for use at a four-year accredited university for the families of Hub Group, Inc., and its subsidiaries. The requirements are:

- A dependent of a Hub Group employee who has completed at least five years of service.
- Applicant to submit a one-page letter, along with a completed application, detailing what the scholarship would mean to them.
- Applicant must have achieved a 3.0 grade point average in secondary school (scale of 4.0) or is presently a student at an accredited university and has maintained a 3.0 grade point average (scale of 4.0).

The scholarship is nontransferable and is for a one-year period. The winner has the opportunity to compete for the award each year he/she remains in school.

### The Joyce E. Yeager Scholarship at the University of Cincinnati

Established in 2001 by Phil to also honor Joyce, this scholarship provides financial assistance to students of Bellevue High School (Kentucky). The requirements are:

- A student of Bellevue High School completing their education in June of the applicable year.
- Applicant to submit a one-page letter, along with a completed application, detailing what the scholarship would mean to them.
- Applicant has achieved a cumulative 3.0 grade point average in secondary school (scale of 4.0).

The scholarship is renewable on a year-to-year basis for completion of undergraduate degree work at the University of Cincinnati (covering a maximum of four years) so long as the student maintains a cumulative 3.0 grade point average (scale of 4.0).[2]

Left: *Inc.* magazine recognized the extraordinary one-year growth of Hub City Indianapolis in 1993, due in great part to Tom Reisinger's successful management of that hub.

Below right: Joe Egertson (left) is pictured with Don Maltby, Jr., at Hub's 25th anniversary bash.

*Inc.* magazine, a publication dedicated to entrepreneurs, recognized this extraordinary growth by including Hub City Indianapolis on its list of the fast-growing companies in the United States for 1993. "After that, we never looked back," Reisinger said. "This was definitely the kind of news the home office was looking to hear."

Not surprisingly, Hub executives attribute much of their success directly to the leadership and management style provided by Phil, David, and Hardin. Inda explained, "There would be these day-long sessions where Phil, David, and Tom would sit together in conference. I think what amazed me about Hub was that those three men did so many things that had a huge success rate. It just amazed me that they had the pulse of the industry. I always felt that we were a year or two ahead of everybody else in the business."[17]

### Launching a Drayage Business

In 1990, Joe Egertson, president of Hub City St. Louis, initiated Hub's in-house drayage company, called Quality Services, LLC, in St. Louis. One of Egertson's biggest challenges involved competition from several IMCs that had drayage programs, as well as J. B. Hunt, which initiated intermodal service at that time.

Egertson and David Beasley, Egertson's operations manager, conceived a program to confront the competition head on. They brought in Jim Ronchetto, a young man with extensive experience in trucking. Within a few months after its development, the

program, called QS, Inc., attracted one of Hub's largest customers, Unilever's St. Louis operation. With Unilever as a client, the program became an immediate success.

As a result, Hub Group decided to proactively expand its drayage business nationally. In January 1995, the leadership team at Hub brought in Dick Rogan, an executive with extensive trucking experience. His freight transportation career began with the Illinois Central Railroad, and then he spent 15 years working for several trucking companies before joining Hub. "They literally hired me to add QS operations to the organization, which we did," said Rogan. QS, Inc., became the Quality Service Division for Hub.

As one of his first orders of business, Rogan decided to bring Ronchetto to Chicago. "I felt that J.R. [Ronchetto] was an outstanding trucker, and I asked him to join me in the effort to add more dray operations to the network," Rogan said.[18]

Moving in a novel direction for Hub, Rogan wanted the new operations to have some of their own company-owned assets. "We recruited a manager in each of the locations we selected (there would be seven under his direction) and went out and bought some tractors, recruited drivers, and started from scratch in each case," Rogan recalled.

# DICK ROGAN

AS A SENIOR EXECUTIVE AND SALES professional with more than 30 years experience, Dick Rogan initially joined Hub Group in 1995 as president of Hub Highway Services. Rogan would help Hub develop its in-house drayage company, Quality Services, LLC, and its newly created brokerage operation. Rogan grew the highway brokerage business from $45 million in 1995 to $215 million in 2001. In addition, he served as executive vice president of sales and marketing from 1999 to 2003. During that time, he developed a logistics strategy, launched an expedited air program, and instituted a national rail car marketing program. In 2004, he took over Hub Group Distribution Services until he retired in 2006.[1]

There would be only one customer for each QS company: Hub. "Hub didn't sell its dray service to other intermodal marketing companies," Rogan explained. Over the following two-and-a-half years, the operations with dray services would grow to include New Jersey, Kansas City, Atlanta, Los Angeles, Chicago, and Grand Rapids, Michigan. Chicago quickly surpassed St. Louis and became the largest market for drayage.[19] With more than 1,200 drivers, Hub has become one of the largest intermodal drayage companies in the United States.[20]

### The NAFTA Effect

On January 1, 1994, President Bill Clinton signed the North American Free Trade Alliance (NAFTA) agreement into law. In 1990, President George H. W. Bush, Canadian Prime Minister Mulroney, and Mexican President de Gortari agreed upon the original alliance. The agreement brought down barriers that previously hindered trade between Mexico, Canada, and the United States due to excessive bureaucracy and duty on products. It also promised to speed up shipping times between the three countries.[21]

Tom Holzmann, Hub Rio Grande president, recalled the anticipation over NAFTA. "We had been very successful at developing the Mexican market and had established operation and sales offices in Laredo and San Antonio, Texas, and Mexico City," he said. "We experienced a challenging set of circumstances as a result of the existing Mexican customs and transportation inconsistencies. Everyone expected that once NAFTA became law, everything would run through in a fluid manner, much like we experience in our domestic freight movements. Unfortunately, that was not quite the case."

Hub Rio Grande did experience an increase in business post-NAFTA as its major clients—including Kraft Foods and Corona Beer—expanded their nonstop intermodal business between Mexico, the United States, and Canada. Holzmann explained, "I used to ship Corona Beer out of Mexico City in containers on trains, and they would go all the way to Chicago. Then we would clear customs in Chicago, and they would go beyond into Canada. NAFTA enabled us to minimize a lot of the stopping and delay that we used to have at the border because the contents had to be taken off the train and inspected. I think NAFTA did what it was intended to do—and that was to increase trade between the countries of the North American continent. It helped us to produce products and be competitive with a lot of other countries around the world that have labor issues, as well as having the ability to make things cheaper."[22]

The signing of the 1994 NAFTA treaty boosted business at Hub Rio Grande, successfully run by Tom Holzmann.

## Hub Creates HLX

The qualified successes that resulted from the NAFTA agreement prompted Hub to create an international division in 1994. "The original vision was to expand our reach to the international marketplace," Hardin said. "Hub was traditionally a domestic shipment company. We felt that we had the infrastructure and the systems to reach out to the international shipping community. Our decision was to actually deal with the steamship lines and the international freight community; that is, the wholesalers. We had the systems and the intermodal expertise to do that."

Hub Group International, or HLX for short, became the name for the international division, and the new venture quickly picked up a lot of foreign business for Hub.[23]

## Hub Goes Public

Moving into the 1990s, David Yeager strategically positioned Hub for a successful future and anticipated a potential problem for its long-term growth. David said:

*We were a graying organization. When I looked at how we were going to transition this business and be fair to the people that created it, and be fair to the company, and be fair to the new people that were going to have to run it moving forward, I couldn't come up with any way to do it other than going public. This was in the era when it was very gung ho. That's when a lot of the truckers had gone public—the Hunts, the Werners, those people. So we began to initiate some discussions with some of the investment bankers, and they felt that we had a very compelling story to go public with.[24]*

When recalling David's urging to go public, Phil commented:

*David's biggest and best idea was to go public, and frankly, I was reluctant. Why should we? We had*

*the biggest and best intermodal company in the country, we were making good money, and we were "debt free." Damn good reasons [not to go public], but David persisted, and finally persuaded Tom and me.*

*It was the best way to go for the following reasons: First, we had secured business from a number of Fortune 500 companies, and these companies wanted to know more about our company— especially if we were their prime carrier. Second, by buying the hubs over several years, we could assist our principals in selling their 25 percent ownership at a good price, and several of our owners were in their upper fifties and were looking for retirement benefits. Third, going public would give us a great deal of good, free publicity.[25]*

Financially rewarding the company's key executives, those early risk takers who had worked so hard and shared the Yeagers' vision over the years, proved the driving force behind Hub's desire to go public. Phil explained, "The reason for going public was very personal. All of our own funds were tied up in the company. Many of our principals were in the same position. Some of them had reached the point in life when they needed a way to retire. We had to do it as a whole company to benefit everyone. We also believed going public would achieve one of our main priorities, which was to get name recognition. There were still a lot of big companies who would not use us because we were not a public company, and they didn't trust the industry."[26]

In addition, Hub hierarchy anticipated that going public would also provide them with a competitive edge. Hardin explained:

*Once we understood more of what being a public company offered us as an organization, we saw*

In 1994, *Distribution Magazine* recognized Hub with its "Quest for Quality" award for the second time for Hub's outstanding service.

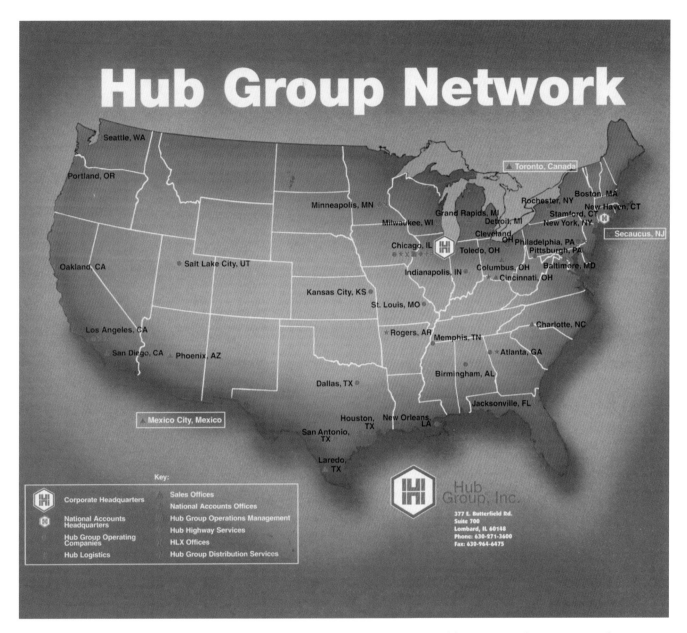

By the mid-1990s, Hub Group had expanded across the United States and included divisions in both Canada and Mexico.

*the merits of that. I guess we felt that we had accomplished all of our goals, and we had a huge company, really, 29 companies out there. Looking at our competitive position in the marketplace, we had some handicaps. We couldn't move as a unit. We didn't have a network. Our vendors and our customers were requiring more of us. Going public would allow us to be more networklike and more*

*single voice–like. As much as we tried to control each operation, it was like herding cats.*"[27]

Hub initiated the process toward going public by incorporating on March 8, 1995. At that time, David became CEO of Hub Group. Other new appointments included Hardin as chief operating officer and a director of the company. Mark became vice president, secretary, and general counsel for Hub Group, while Phil retained the title of chairman of the board.[28]

In a relatively short three years, the Yeager family had dealt with a profound personal loss, and enjoyed professional successes as the second generation of the family moved into increased prominence within Hub Group. Hub had again expanded services to meet client needs, absorbed a once-formidable competitor, and developed a plan to reward its division heads for years of faithful service, while increasing the company's profile by going public. To continue Hub's upward trajectory, its upper management would need to convince the principals at the 29 hubs, along with the investment world of the positive aspects of going public. Those hurdles would come next.

# REMEMBERING JOYCE YEAGER

REMINISCING ABOUT HIS MOTHER, Mark Yeager, Joyce's youngest son, commented:

*While my mom had a number of outstanding attributes, her strength of character was clear to everyone that met her. She knew right from wrong and wasn't afraid to stand up for herself or her family. Being the boss's wife, it was easy for people to underestimate her. But she took her job very seriously and performed it well. If you were smart, you showed her the respect that she'd earned. If you didn't, your future was probably with another company. She was a strong woman at a time when strong women weren't exactly the norm. That was a good thing because transportation was a pretty rough business at the time.*

*At the office, she trusted her instincts and had a great feel for who was going to work hard and contribute and who wasn't a team player. At home, you were expected to do your chores, keep your room clean, and help out around the house.*

*At the same time, she was a very energetic, fun-loving, and generous person. We laughed a lot, sitting out on the front porch in the rain or at the dining room table for family gatherings. She loved being out, whether it was going shopping (the people at her favorite store still talk about her, more than 12 years after her death), out to dinner (three-hour minimum), or sitting in a hotel lobby watching everyone go by. These were things she didn't get to do as a young person, and that made them that much more special.*

*She loved animals, donating to a number of charities and treating our pets like royalty, and made a huge impression on those around her. In fact, my best friend's daughter is named Allison Joy, with the middle name being in honor of my mom.*

*She was also always willing to try new things. I remember my mom, dad, and I learning to ski*

*when I was around 10. She showed up in a fur-collared sweater (it was okay then) and black dress gloves. What made it really funny was that she brought her purse to the slopes and skied with it most of the day. Only my mom could pull that off and make it look good.*[1]

Tom Hardin recalled:

*Joyce and I became friends (over the phone) before I ever met Phil. She was managing the operations at the newly started Hub City, while Phil was out making sales calls. I was running a small shipper agent at the same time, so I spoke with Joyce almost daily as we co-loaded shipments together.*

*We got along great right from the start. I know she had a lot to do with the fact that Phil ultimately hired me as their first employee. At Hub, Joyce and I worked closely together running the "inside," while Phil was "Mr. Outside." It was a great team, and she was a great lady and a great friend.*[2]

Phil Yeager reminisced about his wife and her strong work ethic:

*She was a force. She did it all. If she made a mistake, she would get so angry at herself, but she didn't make many, I'll tell you that. She was very supportive with our customers and our employees. As a business associate, she was tremendous. Everyone told me, "Never work with your wife." Well, we had about 20 Hubs started by husband-and-wife teams, and it worked. Who would work harder? Who would believe in you more than your wife?*

*Joyce was a tireless worker. She did the work of three people, and, boy, was she a perfectionist. She was just a terrific gal and kept me on my toes. She could pat me on the head one day to help build up my ego and the next she could reduce the size of my head if she noticed a "too cocky" attitude.*[3]

4,575,000 SHARES

**Subject To Completion**
February 6, 1996

# Hub Group, Inc.

### CLASS A COMMON STOCK

Of the 4,575,000 shares of Class A Common Stock (the "Class A Common Stock") offered hereby, 3,575,000 shares are being sold by Hub Group, Inc., a Delaware corporation (the "Company" or "Hub Group"), and 1,000,000 shares are being sold by a stockholder of the Company (the "Selling Stockholder"). See "Principal and Selling Stockholders." The Company will not receive any proceeds from the sale of shares by the Selling Stockholder. Prior to this Offering, there has been no public market for the Class A Common Stock. It is currently estimated that the initial public offering price will be between $14.00 and $16.00 per share. See "Underwriting" for a discussion of the factors to be considered in determining the initial public offering price. The Company has applied to have the Class A Common Stock approved for quotation on the Nasdaq Stock Market (National Market) under the symbol "HUBG."

The Company's authorized common stock includes Class A Common Stock and Class B Common Stock (the "Class B Common Stock" and together with the Class A Common Stock, the "Common Stock"). The rights of holders of Class A Common Stock and Class B Common Stock are identical, except each share of Class B Common Stock entitles its holder to 20 votes, while each share of Class A Common Stock entitles its holder to one vote. Upon completion of the Offering, the holders of the Class B Common Stock will control approximately 74% of the total voting power of the Company. Each share of Class B Common Stock converts into one share of Class A Common Stock (i) at any time at the option of the holder and (ii) automatically upon its sale or other transfer to anyone other than Phillip C. Yeager or a member of his immediate family. See "Description of Capital Stock."

**See "Risk Factors" beginning on page 12 for certain information that should be considered by prospective investors.**

THESE SECURITIES HAVE NOT BEEN APPROVED OR DISAPPROVED BY THE SECURITIES AND EXCHANGE COMMISSION OR ANY STATE SECURITIES COMMISSION NOR HAS THE SECURITIES AND EXCHANGE COMMISSION OR ANY STATE SECURITIES COMMISSION PASSED UPON THE ACCURACY OR ADEQUACY OF THIS PROSPECTUS. ANY REPRESENTATION TO THE CONTRARY IS A CRIMINAL OFFENSE.

| | Price to Public | Underwriting Discounts and Commissions | Proceeds to Company(1) | Proceeds to Selling Stockholder |
|---|---|---|---|---|
| | $ | $ | $ | $ |
| Per Share | $ | $ | $ | $ |
| Total(2) | $ | $ | $ | $ |

(1) Before deducting estimated expenses of $1,758,000 payable by the Company.

(2) The Company has granted the Underwriters a 30-day option to purchase up to 686,250 additional shares of Class A Common Stock solely to cover over-allotments, if any. To the extent that the option is exercised, the Underwriters will offer the additional shares to the public at the Price to Public shown above. If the option is exercised in full, the total Price to Public, Underwriting Discounts and Commissions and Proceeds to Company will be $     , $     and $     , respectively. See "Underwriting."

The shares of Class A Common Stock are offered by the several Underwriters, subject to prior sale, when, as, and if delivered to and accepted by them, subject to the right of the Underwriters to reject any order in whole or in part. It is expected that delivery of the shares will be made at the offices of Alex. Brown & Sons Incorporated, Baltimore, Maryland, on or about          , 1996.

ALEX. BROWN & SONS
INCORPORATED

SCHRODER WERTHEIM & CO.

WILLIAM BLAIR & COMPANY

**The date of this Prospectus is**          , 1996.

The cover page of the prospectus offering investors the opportunity to invest in Hub's first public offering in February 1996.

# CHAPTER SIX

# HUB GOES PUBLIC

## 1996–1999

*The culture is always focused on winning here.*

—James Gaw

HAVING MADE THE DECISION to go public, Hub's leadership now needed to sell the concept to many minority owners, along with the investment community. As 1996 began, Phillip, David, and Mark Yeager, along with Tom Hardin and Hub Chief Financial Officer Bill Crowder, spearheaded the process of promoting to the public the long-term investment viability of a third-party intermodal transportation corporation.

The benefits of going public for the company were clear. The real challenge involved convincing all of the hub presidents that they would benefit from the move to go public. The hub presidents were asked to sell at least 30 percent of their holdings in their individual Subchapter S corporations initially, in addition to providing Hub Group with the option to buy the remaining 70 percent at a later date. They would also need to surrender business control of their operation after the company went public, as well as agree to sign a noncompete agreement. "It was sort of a miracle, I think, that it happened," said David Zeilstra, Hub's vice president and general counsel.

At the time, Zeilstra worked for Hub's law firm, Mayer, Brown & Platt. He explained:

*You had more than 20 Subchapter S corporations, all contributing their assets and liabilities to a number of limited partnerships, which were then selling their general partnership interests to the public. It was a very complex deal, because you had not only the public offering but you also had a corporate restructuring that was going on at the same time. I didn't know if this deal would ever get done. Think about getting 50 to 75 separate people to all agree to something. You know, that's not easy to do.*[1]

Dan Hardman, then-president of Hub Chicago, said, "You had 20-something offices and 20-something different ways of doing things and 20-something different agendas, and you had 20-something different guys calling the shots. It was a pretty bold initiative to present to some very entrepreneurial people."[2]

Joe Wallace, Hub Ohio president at the time, recalled, "The initial information was delivered to us at a meeting in Florida, and it was more of a suggestion, 'This is an option that we have out there.' I remember sitting at that meeting, and there was a sense of excitement in the room. I don't think any of the principals had ever con-

---

This 1998 Hub Group Annual Report discussed the company's strategy to gain market share and sustain long-term profitable growth by providing excellent customer service.

sidered that as an option. It was more of a hypothetical. There was a sense of excitement that one, there certainly would be a financial payoff for all of us, and two, that we were going big-time."[3]

The majority of the hub presidents shared Wallace's enthusiasm. Bill Schmidt, then-president of Hub Golden Gate, said: "The idea of going public was appealing to most of us that had been there a long time and understood the culture of Hub, and where we had been, and what we needed to do to go further. There was a real need to develop big capital, and the public offering was a real vehicle to do that."[4]

Jim Decker, Los Angeles Hub president, remembered: "It excited me. I thought it was a great idea. My wife, Nancy, had survived breast cancer, and I had fought off melanoma, and I felt that we were not going to have long lives. I could see myself dying at my desk, so I embraced the idea immediately."[5]

Stanley Dick, Hub's former director of special projects and one of Hub's early employees—he joined the nascent company in 1976, after meeting Phil on an elevator—recalled, "I saw this thing coming a year before they made the change and bought out all the offices. There was too much going on between the offices, they had become too competitive with one another, and it just wasn't good for the company."[6]

Dick's wife, Donna, who started working at Hub in 1976 as assistant to Joyce Yeager, wasn't surprised when she first heard about the decision to go public. Currently the Intermodal Coordinator and Dispatcher for Hub Chicago, she said, "What they've always done is try to improve. Never just sit back and say, 'We're doing good.' You know, they just kept going. 'Okay,' they say. 'What else can we do to make this a better company?'"[7]

The Hub IPO team—which consisted of the Yeagers, Hardin, their CFO Crowder, and the outside legal team of Mayer, Brown & Platt—brought in financial advisory firm Duff & Phelps to help with a valuation analysis. Wallace recalled:

*We all went through interviews with the analysts. One of our strengths, I think the selling feature, was that each of us in our territories knew our marketplace and had a sense of ownership. All of my colleagues had that sense of "this is my busi-*

*ness. I know what's going on," and that was enticing to the investment community.*

*It was very difficult because we were trying to develop a structure that still enabled that flexibility and independence in the field, yet had the legal structure binding us all together. It was probably one of the most complicated deals the investment community had ever seen. But I think that's what they were buying—that uniqueness—and we didn't want to lose that success mechanism.*[8]

Not all the hub presidents came on board immediately. "Some were skeptical," Mark said. "I think some of them embraced it because they recognized the exit strategy benefits for them personally, and some embraced it because they recognized that we needed to be one company. But there were a good number of them who weren't all that thrilled with it. I think we got resistance from folks who were worried that the culture was going to change; that we were going to become a big bureaucracy. But, because it offered liquidity and some benefits to them personally, eventually everyone went along with the program."[9]

Ultimately, Phil's proven integrity served to convince all concerned to agree to the terms of the buyout. Hub North Central President Ron Hazlett said, "It goes back to the way Phil supported it. I don't think it would have ever worked if it hadn't been for Phil's idea of how to accomplish it. He made an awful lot of people wealthy."[10] Zeilstra concurred, "The driving force was definitely the trust that people had in the integrity of the Yeagers. They trusted that it would be a fair deal, and I think it was."[11]

### Convincing the Analysts

With all the various hub division presidents on board with taking the company public, it was time to prepare the offering for outside investors. To do so, the Hub Group IPO team needed to develop a prospectus. Mark commented on the complexity of the process, "I think we drafted the prospectus 58 or 59 different times. It was a delicate IPO environment in 1996. If you timed it right, you could do it, but you really had to have everything lined up. We had such an exotic struc-

Phil Yeager's integrity and reputation helped to convince all the principals of the various hubs to agree to the public offering and the restructuring plans.

ture because we maintained the Subchapter S corporations. We tried to put it on a diagram at one point in the prospectus. It looked like a spider colony, so we decided to try to explain it in words. Even so, it was still very complex."[12]

One important component of the IPO process involves the senior management team meeting with prospective analysts and stock investors, known as the road show. "It's kind of a grueling experience," Phil said.[13] David added, "We knew that if we were on a call to a potential investor, and we started to go into detail on the structure, we might as well leave because there's no way he'd buy it. It was just so complex."

To hold the investor's interest, Hub simplified the presentation by providing a one-page summary, along with a scripted presentation that included their impressive earning statements for the previous three years. David recalled:

*I think there were some questions about structure, but not a tremendous amount. They looked and said, "This is good cash flow. This is an industry that seems to make sense." If there was a concern, it was probably about Hub's long-term viability as a third party: "Are you always going to be in a position to represent the railroads? Do they really need you? How can you make money when you don't own the boxes?" There was always the question about how viable the long-term business model was.[14]*

Hub's team presentation demonstrated that the company brought value to the railroads and to its customers, and that the costs for the railroads to attempt to provide the same services on their own would be prohibitive and ineffective. Phil, in his no-nonsense manner, explained, "We told them what we were going to do, and we told them what we felt the benefits were, and that was that."

The Hub IPO team spent a few weeks on the road traveling throughout the United States and Europe gathering investors. The deal priced out at $14 a share. Phil wasn't thrilled with the price of the stock, "I was perturbed that we didn't get a better price, but then the stock really took off and that was gratifying to see."[15]

On March 18, 1996, Hub Group purchased Hub City Terminals, Inc. (the Chicago office), in a stock-for-stock acquisition. At the same time, Hub completed an initial public offering of 4,261,250 shares of Class A common stock with net proceeds to Hub Group of $52.9 million. Concurrent with the public offering, Hub Group, through its new wholly owned subsidiary, Hub Chicago, acquired with cash the 30 percent general partnership interests in all of the operating Subchapter S corporations, and retained the option to acquire the balance at a later date.[16]

In addition, Hub Group directly acquired a controlling interest in Hub Group Distribution Services, the specialized logistics division of the partnership.[17] In connection with going public, Hub also added three independent directors to its board including: Martin Slark, a senior executive with Molex, Inc.; Gary Eppen, a professor in the Graduate School of Business at the University of Chicago; and Charles Reaves, a retired Sears transportation executive who owns a real estate development company. As Phil noted, "We were extremely fortunate to add three highly intelligent, successful directors to our board. They are all team players and have proven to be a great catalyst for improvement at Hub"[18]

In a March 22, 1996, notice to their members, NASDAQ National Market listed 77 new issues as having joined the NASDAQ. Among them was—HUBG—the newly minted stock symbol for Hub Group. Then on April 19, 1996, Hub celebrated its 25th anniversary.[19]

### Hub Makes an Acquisition

Shortly after its successful IPO, Hub prepared to make a significant acquisition of American President Distribution Services (APDS), a division of American President Lines (APL), the wholesale distribution company that had introduced the first double-stack train in 1984. APL had taken the intermodal industry by storm and became the industry standard but had struggled in developing a successful retail product.

In the spring of 1996, APL elected to sell APDS, and Hub made an offer. "APL was one of our stack train vendors that did a great job service-wise, but couldn't seem to bring enough margins on its retail business to make a profit," Phil said. "Hub always was able to make a profit because we had the most experienced professionals working for us. Our people loved our company and worked hard to satisfy our customers."[20]

Hardin commented, "We had a tremendous relationship with the parent company, APL. Our two companies really, really became very closely aligned over the years. We did a lot of business with those guys. They were our first choice for doing business."

Though other companies made offers, APL accepted Hub's bid, and on May 2, 1996, Hub acquired APDS. Hardin said, "Our bid was unique and obviously the one that prevailed because we had the ability not only to pay a fair cash price but also we could, in fact, guarantee certain business levels back to the stack train."[21]

The details of the deal—which happened in near record time—are striking. Hardin, who oversaw the three-man team for Hub that handled the negotiations recalled:

*This was really a unique scenario. They wanted to get rid of the retail cost, but they wanted to keep the business that it generated. So we devised an innovative approach. We basically said, "Okay, we'll pay you x amount in cash over time, and in addition to that, we'll give you a contractual commitment on the business that your entity generates for you. We'll continue that. You get zero cost and money in your pocket." That's how we did it.*

*They only had a week or so to do this deal, and we worked day and night on it. We set up teleconferences, we faxed back and forth, we worked at home. We had such strong relationships that we could be very honest in the process. I could pick up the phone at night and call their president and their executive vice president at home. They had to get this thing accomplished by a certain date.[22]*

Stephen Cosgrove, Hub's executive vice president of intermodal operations and administration, served on the evaluation team. He joined Hub after working for APL. Cosgrove commented:

*It felt a little weird that Hub was buying my old company. There we were buying a competitor and taking their book of business. It was fun to be part of the evaluation team.*

*Before I came to Hub, I knew all the principals. They just had the winning attitude. It was just a real positive, strong, growth kind of company. You get in a room with a half-dozen or a dozen of the principals, the presidents of the different offices, and you say, "That's just a powerful group." And Phil Yeager was the example at the top.[23]*

In signing the deal, Hub acquired the right to service APDS customers but didn't assume any assets or liabilities from the business. In order to complete the venture, Hub hired 36 of the APDS employees experienced in intermodal operations. The combined estimated 1995 revenues for Hub and APDS exceeded $800 million.[24]

In one fell swoop, Hardin estimated that Hub realized almost $100 million worth of new business. "I think the key to that involved two things. First, we were able to negotiate that quickly, and second, we were able to assimilate the business into our business very fluidly. We hadn't done it before, but we got our respective teams together,

# HUB CELEBRATES 25 YEARS

H UB'S ANNUAL THREE-DAY GATHERING of executives took on a festive air in 1996. On April 19, Hub commemorated its 25th anniversary with a banquet hosted by the Yeagers at the Oak Brook Hills Resort in Oak Brook, Illinois.[1] "It was a wonderful occasion to celebrate because, in addition to all of our presidents who came in for the meeting, we had their wives and some very special guests. We were having a tremendous year both in volume growth and profit," Phillip Yeager recalled.[2] The special guests included many longtime Hub clients and railroad executives who toasted Hub and wished them well as Hub planned for its future successes.[3]

Besides celebrating 25 years in business, Hub colleagues and clients had the opportunity to share a meal and a laugh with associates otherwise scattered across the United States. Left to right, top row: Tom Mull, Jim Gaw; Tom and Bonnie Hardin; Mark Diamond, David Marsh; David Yeager, Phil Yeager. Second row: John Donnell, Jim Gaw; Don Deese; Dan Hardman, Glen Meadows. Third row: Mark Smith, Bill Crowder; Pat Sweeney. Bottom row: Bob Weaver, Phil Bayle.

and what was good about it was that the cultures of the two companies fit. It was like putting Pepsi in a Coca-Cola bottle. It's all the same deal."

The end result provided continued momentum for Hub. Hardin said, "This was another stepping-stone for Hub's growth. It was a great, great success story—kind of a main event in the progression of our company. We've always come up with something big at the right time, and the acquisition of APDS was a big one."[25]

### Mega Mergers

Since the government's deregulation of the rail industry in 1980, the financially troubled railroads had adopted several methods in order to survive. The merger mania of the 1990s served as a survival tactic, which was wholeheartedly embraced by the industry. In September 1995, two giant railroads, the Burlington Northern and the Santa Fe joined forces to become BNSF, creating the first major railroad consolidation in the West. This Fort Worth, Texas–based giant had estimated revenues of $8 billion and 31,000 miles of track.[26]

Hub's current senior vice president of intermodal, Brian Avery, said, "Of all the mergers and acquisitions, that one probably had the most prolonged impact on service."[27] Hardin agreed, "They suffered a bit service-wise. They found it a little bit of a different world when you try to consolidate a northern railroad and a southern railroad in the West. It's a different landscape. But in any event, we persevered, and they persevered, and now they're again the most efficient intermodal railroad in the world."[28]

A year later, on September 11, 1996, two of its major competitors answered the BNSF merger with their own consolidation. The Union Pacific Railroad merged with the Southern Pacific (SP). The newly formed Union Pacific (UP) then became the largest railroad in the United States with 36,000 miles of track. In less than a year, the UP merger would have an adverse effect on the entire intermodal community by causing a major service crisis, and this time, Hub would experience negative repercussions.[29]

### Hub Continues to Consolidate

The Yeagers always intended to buy back the hub divisions as part of their overall plan, partly to reward the long-standing hub presidents, many of whom had reached retirement age. These executives had the option of staying on at their posts after the initial 30 percent Hub Group purchase. But, one by one, the division heads opted for retirement.[30] As a result, Hub began the process of buying back the remaining 70 percent of its partnerships. First, Hub purchased Hub Tennessee in August 1996, then Hub North Central in December of that year.[31]

In some cases, these purchases prompted a changing of the guard. Hazlett, president of Hub North Central and Hub's first salesman hired by Phil in 1973, recalled: "I took the original buyout, and I stayed on for a little while, then retired in early 1997. Jim Gaw was my successor in Milwaukee, and he's now the executive vice president of sales. I could have stayed, but it just seemed like the time had come to retire, and I'm grateful to Phil. He made an awful lot of people successful."[32]

As 1997 began, Hub confronted challenges typical of a company in transition. Former hub principal Wallace said, "The rigors and changes in culture, processes, structure, and reporting in the new 'public' company were probably underestimated and, as a result, the organization struggled to adapt. Not surprisingly, because of the dynamic personalities and previous success, it was a difficult adjustment. We really were a company in transition that had lost some of its identity."

At a critical crossroad, Hub attempted to adapt to its new environment while utilizing its original management formula, which had proven so successful. At the same time, industry costs skyrocketed, due in part to the railroad mergers. This adjustment period created stress and anxiety for the company and its employees.

"This was a dangerous and vulnerable time for Hub," Wallace recalled, "I'm sure it was as difficult a time for Phil and Dave Yeager as it was for the entire organization. What Phil had spent 30 years building was now changing. They had to strike the correct balance between providing more structure and leadership, and improving communication in the field."[33]

Throughout 1997, Hub continued its consolidation plan by making strategic investments. On March 1, Hub acquired an additional 44 percent ownership interest in Hub Distribution Services for $1.5 million, raising its stake to 65 percent.[34]

According to Schmidt, former president of Hub Golden Gate, "By the fall of 1997, I believed that the value of my company was as good as it was going to get, and all the other criteria fell into place." He decided it would be a great time to sell his ownership back and retire.[35] Decker, president of Hub Los Angeles felt the same way. Both had watched Hazlett and other hub presidents sell their ownership and retire comfortably, and now they felt the time had come for them to do the same.[36]

The Yeagers and Hardin agreed with the timing, but it would take a second public offering to raise the money to buy back the remaining percentages in the highly profitable Golden Gate and Los Angeles hubs.

### Raising Capital

A second public offering occurred in September 1997, and netted approximately $54.8 million with an issuance of 1,725,000 shares of stock. By this time, Hub's stock was at $38 a share, it had really taken off. Unfortunately, when the UP and SP merger occurred, the stock dropped dramatically, despite the fact that the company was showing a 27 percent increase in volume and profits."[37]

Having experienced and survived multiple railroad mergers in the past, Hub and the rest of the intermodal industry expected a quick resolution to the UP service problems. Undeterred, Hub opened a $36 million, five-year revolving line of credit with Harris Trust and Savings Bank in order to finalize the purchase of the Golden Gate and Los Angeles partnerships and provide much needed working capital. Unfortunately, the UP Service problem lingered, and for the first time in its history, Hub acquired debt.[38]

### The Union Pacific "Meltdown"

One of Hub's greatest assets from its outset had been its close relationships with the railroads, the backbone of the intermodal industry. Most of the original hub principals had railroad experience, as did Phil and Tom. But the merger of the Union Pacific and Southern Pacific created service slowdowns that were unprecedented in the industry. "In 40 years in the business, I never saw anything like it. I mean, not even close," Phil said about the situation.[39]

Why did the "meltdown" occur? Both the Union Pacific and Southern Pacific railroads, huge entities on their own, had trouble adapting to the merger at some very basic levels. For example, the computer systems between the two railroads were incompatible. Unsettled labor agreements existed restricting crew flexibility, and inadequate locomotive power led to gridlock throughout the rail system.[40] Phil recalled, "It was like a snowball, it started out small, and it got bigger and bigger and bigger. Finally, it affected not only the UP railroad, but all the railroads. We had equipment problems because they weren't getting efficient utilization, we had car problems and trailer problems. It was a huge mess."[41]

An article in the *San Francisco Chronicle* in the fall of 1997 called it the corporate merger from hell, and vividly described the gridlock problems caused by the merged railroads: "The rail gridlock began with paralysis in a switching yard in Houston and spread all over the West like a disease. It affected coal shipments in Colorado, grain in the Midwest, shipments of frozen French fries from Idaho to Japan, automobile parts, Amtrak passenger trains, even shipping containers full of stuffed animal toys bound from China for the Christmas market."[42]

On average, the Union Pacific carried 350,000 carloads of freight. The gridlock problems caused those carloads to sit, unable to make progress. It would take months to resolve the logjam— well into 1998—which shook up the entire intermodal industry.[43]

Hardin commented on the challenging aspects of the merger as well. "It was a real problem and it created a meltdown. Gridlock. You could not get through the system no matter who you were. You could have been General Motors or United Parcel. It didn't matter. It was a nightmare, and the headache lasted a long time."[44]

Hub did what it could to expedite shipments and appease anxious customers. Phil explained:

*It was a situation that got out of hand. We lost a lot of customer confidence in both the railroads and even sometimes in us. About halfway through the UP merger problem, our customers were very upset. During that period, we actually brought on more than 100 additional people, strictly to serve the customers, at a very heavy expense for us. But we thought that it was necessary to do every-*

*thing possible for them and keep them informed on services.*

*Many times, we had to tell them that we couldn't do fourth morning to the West Coast. We couldn't do second morning to the East Coast. "This is what it is: five days to the West Coast, three days to the East Coast." Many times, by being honest with them, they at least had alternatives.*

*They could put it on a truck or they could try to ship it a day or two early. I think operating on that basis, even though we estimated that we lost more than $100 million worth of business during that period, eventually it came back. So being honest with the customer made a difference in the long run.*

The Union Pacific Railroad worked hard to resolve many of its service issues. By 1998, it had improved its service and exceeded industry records for volume shipping.[45]

David Yeager dubbed the fallout from the Union Pacific and Southern Pacific merger debacle a meltdown. The merger of the railroads caused unprecedented gridlock problems nationwide.

### A Hub Landmark

Although the UP gridlock hurt Hub financially, it didn't forestall Hub's continued consolidation and growth. On October 31, 1997, Hub exercised its option to acquire the remaining 70 percent interest in the New Orleans operation for a nominal sum. It also bought the remaining 50 percent interest in HLX for $300,000, taking full control of the international division that had previously existed as a joint venture.[46]

Then, on December 9, 1997, Hub achieved a remarkable goal. It reached the $1 billion mark in sales. This was despite tremendous service problems brought on by several rail mergers during the mid-1990s, which made the achievement all the more remarkable.[47] To commemorate the occasion, Phil sent every Hub employee a bronze medallion, displayed in an acrylic plaque and inscribed with the momentous date. Harry Inda, Hub's office manager recalled, "That was a very memorable milestone. I thought to myself, 'Man alive, this is a billion-dollar company that started out of one little office.' That was just amazing."[48]

It was a perfect way to cap off an extraordinary year—and a precursor to more positive growth ahead.

### More Acquisitions, More Growth

As 1998 began, Hub faced some significant business challenges. "Costs were going up, demand for services had flattened, and competition for the business was fierce," Phil said. "We had entered a period where we were still profitable, but rapid growth in sales and profit was over. We had always gauged our goals for the coming year based on at least double the industry's forecast. The service problem showed us that, one, we had to diversify product, and two, we needed to be able to control equipment without purchasing it."[49]

But first, Hub needed to acquire control of more of its local operating companies. On March 10, the company announced its intention to acquire the remaining 70 percent minority interest in Hub City Rio Grande, Hub City Dallas, and Hub City Houston, at a cost of approximately $6 million. After the completion of these acquisitions, all hubs in Texas, as well as Mexico, became wholly owned by Hub Group. Phil said, "These acquisitions will help the company improve efficiency and provide a greater level of service to our customers by transporting freight in and out of the Texas and Mexico markets."[50]

Two days after this announcement, Hub disclosed to the media its intention to purchase the outstanding stock of Quality Intermodal Corporation, a trucking and intermodal brokerage service. Headquartered in Houston, Quality Intermodal Corporation had offices in Dallas, Los Angeles, Chicago, Philadelphia, and Atlanta. In 1997, Quality boasted revenues of approximately $70 million.[51] Hub purchased Quality Intermodal Corporation's stock for $4.1 million in cash, plus $6.2 million through the issuance of a three-year note. Hub absorbed the Quality business into its own operations. The purchase offered Hub a much greater presence in the Texas and Mexico transportation market.[52]

Hub's decision to diversify its business beyond intermodal paid off at the outset of the service crisis with the UP. The company's Highway Services Division handled 125,000 truckloads annually at the time of the crisis, and, in the words of Hardin: "Ramped up to meet the challenge." As a result, Hub's Intermodal Division was the last to suffer from the congestion and was the first to recover at the end of 1997 when the service slowdown finally began to resolve itself.[53]

Hub's close relationship with the railroads would help it avoid much of the UP fallout. Hardin told *Traffic World* magazine, "Hub has been coping with the situation by using alternative rail routes, such as going through Kansas City instead of Chicago, and relying on Hub's own truck brokerage division to pick up the slack."[54]

The intermodal industry as a whole did not escape from the service slowdown unscathed. During the period of the crisis, the highly competitive trucking industry stepped in to fill the void, and the trucking industry experienced an impressive growth of 20 percent as a result.[55]

### The Premier Service Network

It was becoming clear that asset-based truck lines, such as J. B. Hunt, were receiving more favorable treatment from BNSF because they furnished their own equipment. In spring 1998, a single meeting would force Hub to reconsider its tra-

ditional non-asset based philosophy. Hardin set up a meeting with BNSF Chairman Robert Krebs to discuss the situation. Krebs, though amenable to a conference, suggested that his vice president of intermodal, Chuck Schultz, join the meeting.

When asked why Hub's competitor received more favorable pricing, Schultz replied, "It's pretty simple. We make a lot more money handling their loads than we do a Hub load because they bring the equipment and Hub doesn't." Hardin explained, "Krebs turned to me and said, 'Tom, I think you've got a problem. You'd better get yourself some equipment.'"[56]

Steve Branscum, BNSF's vice president of intermodal said, "We were seeing that the assets that the motor carriers were bringing to the table were moving through our system at a much faster pace. We were getting more loads per piece of equipment than the non-asset guys were getting out of the equipment that we were providing to them. They weren't sitting around as long in our terminals in an idle

Before joining Hub, David Zeilstra worked for Hub's law firm, Mayer, Brown & Platt. He now serves as vice president and general counsel at Hub.

After Hub exceeded $1 billion in sales, Phil Yeager credited his employees for this outstanding achievement and sent out this announcement that he personally signed.

On December 9, 1997, Hub Group, Inc. reached a historic milestone by topping the $1 billion mark in sales. During the 26 years between the founding of the company and this major accomplishment, Hub Group grew from a single office with two employees into the largest IMC in North America because of the dedication and contribution of our employees.

As a token of my appreciation, I am pleased to present you with this award commemorating our achievement. Thank you for your "Excellence in Execution".

Sincerely,

*Phillip C. Yeager*

Phillip C. Yeager, Chairman

manner. So all the signals and all the measures that we were seeing from testing the waters with the motor carrier community, as opposed to the non-asset community, were telling us it was a better model."[57]

Hardin knew that in order to retain the BNSF railroad—one of the cornerstones of Hub's intermodal business—Hub executives would need to come up with a solution quickly. Hardin recalled, "We sat up all night long thinking about different scenarios. Good heavens, did we have to go out and buy equipment? We needed millions of dollars. Phil Yeager will never do that. It's going to be $100 million to bring this equipment. What are we going to do?"

Finally Hardin hit on an idea. "Going back to my early origins, the first company that I worked for, the roots of that business was piggyback, and they leased the trailer as a separate transaction from the railroad. I said, 'Hey, what if we lease the equipment from the BNSF and put our name on it? Maybe we'd be entitled to favorable rates because it would be treated as private equipment.'"[58]

Hardin took his idea to an informal meeting with BNSF's Branscum. "I purposely went into that meeting without any files, paper, just nothing,"

Hardin recalled. "I said, 'Steve, let's just talk today, and if you think this idea has merit, I'd like to progress it.'"

Branscum acknowledged that BNSF now favored asset-based trucking companies, which would leave Hub "pretty much near the bottom of the totem pole," Hardin recalled. But when Hardin presented his idea of leasing BNSF equipment and putting Hub's name on it, Branscum's face lit up. The railroad wanted to divest itself from the responsibility of handling its own containers. Hardin's plan would allow Hub to continue to maintain its treasured asset-free status, while controlling the containers of a key transportation partner.[59]

The discussions resulted in a win-win proposition. In late April 1998, Hub announced the introduction of its Premier Service Network. The program would involve Hub leasing 2,000 containers from BNSF. Hub would initially lease 1,000 of the 48-foot containers (then the industry standard) from BNSF's fleet, with another 1,000 additional containers coming online from BNSF in October 1998, accounting for roughly 10 percent of BNSF's total fleet.[60] Branscum told *Traffic World* magazine:

*We've all said that we needed to improve utilization if we were going to continue to invest in intermodal equipment. Hub jumped up and said, "We're going to deal with that." It was a bold move on their part. The Hub Group came to us with suggestions of how to do a program. They have the incentive to move the equipment faster to increase utilization, increase revenue, and improve service to customers.*

Brian Avery commented, "The key to success for Hub Group's Premier Service Network is the high degree of differentiation and reliability it will offer customers. This intermodal concept comes at a time when customer demands for service, reliability, and equipment availability have never been greater."

Hardin noted, "We are doing what we do best, which is manage the equipment. This is also an opportunity to recapture business that has been lost due to rail service problems. Having the entire 2,000 units available by October will enable Hub to have a better fleet available in the fall, the traditional period of intermodal equipment shortages."[61]

In the years to come, the Premier Service Network would become one of the company's most successful ventures, expanding to other railroads and growing to more than 13,000 containers. "I'm kind of proud of that one," Hardin conceded. "But it certainly helped that I had been in the business a long time and remembered the original piggyback trailer leasing thing."[62]

While working so closely with Hardin's team on formulating the Premier Service Network, BNSF's Branscum was duly impressed with Hub Group professionalism. "There are two things that

As a memento and thank you gift, Phil Yeager sent every Hub employee this keepsake plaque commemorating Hub Group's milestone of exceeding $1 billion in sales.

I think made Hub different. They were always the most professional organization in terms of their approach to selling. Second, they've been the most willing to take some risk, and accept change, and set themselves up to continue to not only exist, but to thrive, and grow, and survive, for the future. They've made some big, bold steps out in the marketplace, and I think positioned themselves well for the future."

### Additional Expansion

Hub continued to expand—both in the United States and abroad—throughout the balance of 1998.[74] Regarding the expansion, Phil commented,

The Premier Service Network program allowed Hub to exclusively lease BNSF containers and proved an immediate success for Hub.

"As we have seen needs, particularly shipper needs, we met those needs and diversified. Going into international was a very important step."[63]

In August 1998, Hub also acquired the rights to service the customers of Corporate Express Distribution Services (CEDS). This acquisition allowed Hub Group Distribution Services to take over CEDS's niche logistics services, including its pharmaceutical sample delivery operation.[64]

The acquisition further bolstered Hub's logistics division and continued its policy of diversification beyond total reliance on intermodal. "We are very strong in intermodal, we are very strong in trucking, and we are learning to develop a strong logistic service to our customers. We are emphasizing logistics to small and mid-size companies that don't have the transportation specialists needed in today's market," Phil said.[65]

### Industry Recognition

By the start of 1999, Hub had persevered through the slowdown caused by the railroad mergers, had continued its expansion into other services, and had launched its successful and ingenious Premier Service Network program. For Phil, the year ended on a high professional note.

Though Phil and Hub earned many awards and recognitions over the years, those given out by the Intermodal Association of North America (IANA), the intermodal industry's leading trade association, held special significance. Hub had received the Intermodal Achievement Award in 1991 from the IANA, and now, in November 1998, the IANA presented Phil with its Silver Kingpin Award. Constance Sheffield, IANA member services and business development vice president, said, "It's a very prestigious award and is given to an individual who is being recognized for exceptional long-term contributions and the impact they've had on the intermodal freight transportation industry." In Sheffield's memory, no other individual has earned the honor of both the Silver Kingpin and the Intermodal Achievement Award.[66]

Commenting on the recognition and Hub's resilient leadership spearheaded by Phil's example, Sheffield said:

*I think Hub's ability to diversify, to reinvent, has sustained and grown its business. Hub also builds relationships between both the carriers and the customers. I think, a lot of the IMC business is a relationship business, and Hub employees are masters of it in terms of marrying the capabilities of the carriers with the requirements of their customers. In our business, it's all about service, and the value-added service that IMCs like Hub provide is the distinguishing characteristic between the companies that fail and those that succeed.*[67]

About Phil Yeager the man, Thomas J. Malloy, vice president of the IANA's member services and business development department commented, "I think that in knowing Phil personally, and also being a competitor for a couple of years, that Phil saw a longer-term vision, and it was a very small group of folks that had that vision. Obviously, Phil's vision was to see how coordination could be done, as most of the original IMC founders did. They were usually former rail employees that were somewhat frustrated at the management style of the railroads at that time. They went on their own and said, 'We can put this together. We can pull a door-to-door movement together, help coordinate, work directly with the shippers,' and I think that vision is noteworthy. Those individuals that took advantage of that are the ones that certainly had the foresight to see where we're going today."[68]

In February 1999, Phil received yet another prestigious honor—that of Transportation Person of the Year—by the New York Traffic Club. Lillian Barrone, director of port commerce for the Port Authority of New York and New Jersey had worked closely with Hub and Phil over the 13 years of her tenure. "Hub always stood out in terms of efficiency, communication, and relationships. Hub's terminal facilities were always viewed as a model of the kind of operations that companies ought to be providing. Second, they were very active as communicators and marketers, not just of their own products, but of the port broadly, and that was a very positive relationship. Third, they were individuals you could count on. You know, they had a great deal of trust and integrity, and that was Phil Yeager's example."[69]

## The Last Roll Up

Since going public and experiencing its first public offering in 1996, Hub had methodically and deliberately sought to gain full ownership of the remaining limited partnerships. Still, in 1999, Hub did not fully own several of those corporations. David described this situation in the early spring of 1999:

*It got to a point where half were in, half were not, and it appeared to us that there was the potential that we were going to run into conflicts of interest. We still had our Sub S holdings, and we had the public entity. So we said the heck with that. We have to go all in. We took out $110 million in debt, and in April 1999, bought out all the Sub S entities that remained.*[70]

In announcing the deal to the media, Phil said, "The acquisition of our remaining 17 operating companies is an attempt to align the company's services, as senior management of various divisions retire. Besides, the business has changed such that seamless cooperation between all operations is needed. The business used to be very transaction driven. Now, 40 percent of our business is with Fortune 500 companies, negotiating thousands of moves."[71]

The principals at the 17 outstanding operations became Hub Group employees and kept their current positions. "Our strength has always been our management at the local level and we expect this move to make us even better," Phil added.

Moving forward as one company would make good business sense in the long run, but the large debt—something the company had never experienced before—created financial concerns for the company. "At the time, based on cash flows, we felt that was not going to be tremendously difficult to deal with," Mark recalled. "It later became like an anchor around our necks and really was a problem."[72]

Hub general counsel Zeilstra said, "I think we believed, and the Yeager family believed, it was the right thing to do, and that it was the right time to do it. I think there was some trepidation about doing that, and quite a bit of discussion around the need for debt, because obviously you have a choice between debt and equity, but it was decided that debt was the best way to go."[73] David agreed, "Phil hates debt. He keeps all his money stuffed in his mattress. But in the end, it was the best way to go."[74]

For better or worse—Hub Group would now proceed in business as a large single entity. Buying back all the Subchapter S companies additionally benefited Hub when it intended to expand its Premier Service Network across the board to other railroads.

In June 1999, CSX railroad and Norfolk Southern purchased Conrail. Hardin said, "There were terrible service problems. Trying to absorb the different networks, different cultures, different ways of doing business."[75]

Avery said about the merger, "I think it was so challenging because, first of all, you had two arch competitors splitting up a railroad, and that would

---

Phil married Anne Springer in 1999 and found a second chance at happiness after seven years as a widower.

be a little tricky certainly. They had to decide who got what. There wasn't a model to refer to for doing that. They ended up with a lot of jointly operated facilities, and that was pretty challenging."[76]

After the Conrail purchase, only four major rail networks existed in the United States: BNSF, UP, CSX, and Norfolk Southern.[77] BNSF was so pleased with the success of Hub's unique "HUBU" program, that it extended its multi-year agreement with Hub. Norfolk Southern's interest in the program served as the impetus for the expansion of the Premiere Service Network. Hardin said, "This program was so successful at BNSF that the NS wanted to get in on it, too. So they put some containers in play. This program allows us the best pricing on the railroad, the best service on the railroad, and higher profit margins than we had in our other business."

By the end of the year, Hub's total fleet would be nearing 5,000 late-model, low-maintenance, 48- and 53-foot containers. These containers were dedicated exclusively to Hub customers and were fully interchangeable between the participating carriers. Hardin commented:

> *Our customers love it. They love it. I think if you asked Phil, Dave, or Mark Yeager what single event has happened at Hub to change the course of our company, everyone would say it's definitely what we call the HUBU program.*[78]

### New Beginnings

On April 10, 1999, Phil embarked on a new chapter in his personal life when he married Anne Springer in Longboat Key, Florida, where the Yeager family routinely vacationed.[79] Anne and Phil met at Hub years earlier, where she and her husband Dan D'Ascanio ran Hub Tennessee. In 1994, Anne's husband passed away, and Anne retired from the business six months later. At a mutual friend's wedding, Anne and Phil reconnected.

"We dated for several years and were engaged for over a year," said Phil. "It was a beautiful wedding with just families, Tom and Bonnie Hardin, Ron and Bobbie Hazlett, and a few other close friends."

The couple, who traveled abroad frequently, opted for a different kind of adventure by honeymooning at fun-filled Disney World.[80]

**Important Acknowledgments**

Tom Hardin came up with the idea for the container-leasing program called the Premier Service Network, which would become one of Hub's most successful ventures.

In July 1999, in recognition of his increased involvement in the company, Mark became the company's president of field operations.[81] Phil said, "We went through a rather extensive reorganization, and in that reorganization, we found that there were certain areas that we did not have enough top staff to take over some of these duties. I think Mark was certainly the individual in the company that fit the needs that we had."

During this period, Phil prepared to participate in a historic event—a first for the intermodal industry—The Intermodal Founding Fathers of North America Conference, which was held from July 27 to 29, 1999, in Aspen, Colorado. Phil, as a bona fide legend in the industry, participated extensively in the conference and made a detailed presentation for a panel dedicated to early intermodal pioneers.[82]

Phil had initially planned to travel to Europe at the time of the conference, but he altered his plans when he received an invitation to participate in this important event sponsored by the University of Denver's Intermodal Transportation Institute. In his acceptance letter Phil commented, "I wouldn't miss it for anything."[83]

Phil spoke on a first-name basis to many of the participants, including longtime business associates and competitors in the industry as well as friends and

One of Hub's clients, the Philadelphia-based BDP International, a leader in global logistics, recognized Hub with its Outstanding Service Award in 1999. The honor acknowledged Hub's superior dedication, commitment, and customer service to BDP.

industry colleagues. Phil proudly took his place alongside the other founding fathers of the intermodal industry. In one of his speeches, he emphasized that the road ahead for intermodal was unlimited.[84]

As 1999 came to a close, results would show that all of Hub's service offerings achieved profitable growth in that year, with net income rising 21.8 percent to $10.8 million, while revenue increased 13.2 percent to $1.3 billion. The Intermodal Services Division produced the largest revenue for the company, while both the Highway Services and Distribution Service divisions posted healthy increases. Hub gained market share in all business segments and predicted in its annual report a bright outlook for the coming year: "We have significant opportunities to further expand and diversify our services."[85]

But, unbeknownst to Hub at the time, its immediate future would be dominated by serious challenges that would threaten its very existence.

# INTERMODAL FOUNDING FATHERS

PHILLIP YEAGER BEGAN HIS presentation at the Intermodal Founding Fathers of North America Conference in Aspen, Colorado, in July 1999 with these words: "I recently read a wonderful article by Gil Carmichael in the April 26, 1999, issue of *Traffic World,* where Gil states that he has heard it said that 'the 20th century's three most important transportation innovations are the airplane, the diesel engine, and intermodal service.' I would have put intermodal service first."[1]

The conference, a three-day gathering of intermodal professionals, was sponsored by the University of Denver and included the Intermodal Founding Fathers Oral History Program.

This program endeavored to document the experience of the originators of this unique profession. Members of the Oral History Program extensively interviewed conference participants and created an archival database as part of an ongoing project. In addition to participating at that level, Phil, often dubbed the father of intermodal, made a presentation as part of an Early Developers Panel.[2]

Other pioneers of the intermodal industry who served on the panel included: A. Daniel O'Neal, former chairman of the ICC and now of PowerTech Toolworks, Inc., a specialized computer consulting and training company; and George Lowman of GATX Corporation, a service-based asset company specializing in transportation and distribution equipment.

Phil provided an overview of his career, challenges met and faced by the industry, and a forecast for the future. After Phil's opening remarks, he related highlights of his spectacular career. "In 1959 when I started, the railroads handled less than a million trailers and containers. Now, in 1999, they carry more than nine million. When four or five of the U.S. railroads started intermodal in 1954, I thought this was the railroad of the future, and I still believe that."[3]

Phil talked about starting Hub in 1971, after 19 years with the railroad, and how he grew the company through husband-and-wife teams:

*I decided that I really wanted to try something on my own, and I knew a little bit about the shipper-agent industry. The original hub had about $10,000 at the start-up—all that I had. It was a tough, tough situation for a number of years, but eventually, in 1975, we started to expand. It took 17 years to complete the network, but Hub is in practically every major city.*

In typical Yeager fashion, Phil gave credit to his associates, to hard work, and to luck: "There are many rewards from working in this business, including a great relationship with my wife."[4]

Phil forecasted success for intermodal companies that still emphasize service and price. "Price is still number one. This will never change, but I hope shippers learn that it's value of service that provides the greatest reduction in cost. Price is only a small part of the equation."

In looking back over his laudable career, Phil concluded, "After 28 years, it's still fun."[5]

During July 1999, Phil Yeager, often referred to as the father of intermodal, actively participated in the Intermodal Founding Fathers of North America Conference in Aspen, Colorado.

# An unsurpassed network linked by technology, powered by expertise

## Hub provides simplicity and confidence — bringing dynamic and flexible solutions to Intermodal shipping.

Hub Group pioneered the concept of the intermodal marketing company. It streamlined the entire intermodal shipping process through optimum routing, scheduling, pricing, and other value-added services.

# CHAPTER SEVEN

# OPPORTUNITIES FOR ADVANCEMENT

## 2000–2003

*Admittedly there were some difficult times, although we always felt very positive about our company. We all knew we had incredible strategic value. I mean … we're Hub.*

—Tom Hardin

BY THE DAWNING OF THE new millennium, the United States had become increasingly focused on technology with millions of Americans hooked on the Internet as early as 1997. Suddenly, companies could directly reach unlimited consumers by way of this new technology, while viewers could browse or shop the information highway at their leisure. Wall Street quickly became the heated center of the dot-com boom. Speculative trading in Internet-based stocks raised the market to its highest level in decades. Dozens of nascent Internet-related companies raised millions of dollars based on little more than a flashy prospectus and predictions of dazzling success.[1]

In a new age that found computers in almost every home, office, and school, companies with a large Internet presence expected to reap the benefits of this new technology. Hub, with a commitment to remain on the cutting edge of advancements in service, recognized that the Internet could add value to its business. Serving as logistic providers for the freight transportation industry, Hub wanted to utilize up-to-the-minute shipment tracking information and other specialized services that the Internet could provide. Mark Yeager commented:

*This is a very tough business. So, every aspect of the transaction requires tremendous diligence and focus. You have to have a lot of discipline, and you have to be really buttoned down to make money in this business, because the margins are so narrow. You have to be tough. You have to be demanding. You have to have high expectations or else you will not be in business. You have to be ready to compete and look for what can give you the competitive edge. We believed that investing in technology could give us that competitive edge.*[2]

Though saddled with heavy debt incurred by completing the buyout of all its divisions, Hub would now need to invest in Web-based technology to connect with its vendors and customers, and to keep the corporation ahead of its competition.[3]

The intricacies of transporting thousands of containers cross-country, through various modes of transportation, had long made computer technology a valuable tool for the industry, which had utilized applications such as electronic data interchange (EDI). Hub's entrepreneurial structure had produced some unique technological challenges of its own. Mark explained, "Historically, while we were all operating off the same software, we had 28 differ-

Hub Group provides comprehensive intermodal, truckload, international, and logistic services by way of a network of 30 offices throughout the United States, Mexico, and Canada.

ent systems. There might be five hubs doing business with Nabisco, and each had its own reference number for the company, so you couldn't retrieve information in any way. We needed a proprietary system for intermodal and highway. We knew we had to build those capabilities because there really wasn't an off-the-shelf product for that."[4]

Hub Chief Information Officer Dennis Polsen concurred, "Frankly, there was no such thing as an intermodal software package that would be available. It just didn't exist. We've always kidded that if you were trying to start a software business selling a system for intermodal companies, you'd sell one or two of them, and then you'd be out of business. There's not that large of a demand." Hub would have to build its own, and to do that, the company brought in Polsen in March 2000. Before joining Hub, Polsen spent about 14 years with trucking giant Schneider National, specializing in systems technology.

Inset: Hub Highway provides local or long-distance services with carriers who are prequalified to provide on-time, problem-free deliveries.

Below: In January 2000, Hub President and COO Tom Hardin (right) was elected chairman of the Intermodal Association of North America, an honored position within the intermodal industry's major trade organization. Hardin replaced Chuck Shultz, vice president of intermodal for BNSF Railway, the outgoing chairman.

"Hub was starting to invest seriously in new technology when they hired me, and they were trying to work and focus on a really centralized approach to their business," Polsen recalled. "They were obviously very decentralized, and that had been very successful for the company, but I think the market had changed as had the competition. The whole landscape had changed in the railroad industry, and I think they were smart enough to recognize that fundamental changes and investments had to be made in order for them to continue to be successful and compete."[5]

Polsen's first order of business involved updating and electronically connecting the 28 divisions with a new computer system called the Transaction Processing System, or TPS for short. "Not a very imaginative name," Mark said. "But it would enable us to connect everyone and manage the company as a single entity."[6]

The new system would focus on centralization. "They were very much aware of the shortcomings of the system that they had written in the past," Polsen said. "TPS would have the ability to view things across the entire network and take a more global network approach to transportation. You have to have a view of the entire world, which is critical in any transportation environment."

Encouraging the divisions to use and support the new system wouldn't be easy. "Frankly, my role was to run interference," Polsen admitted. "There were 28 separate worlds. It was tough because obviously these companies were very successful initially because every market had its own niche. They had their own customer base. As truckload carriers started to get into the intermodal business, they had a more global view of things. Hub recognized early on it needed to take a global approach as well."[7]

### Hub Invests in Technology

The price tag for the IT investment would be a staggering $50 million. Polsen put the figure in perspective:

Above: Don Maltby, Jr., headed up Hub's e-commerce division in 1998 and oversaw the successful revamping of Hub's Web site in January 2001.

Left: Innovative thinking enabled Hub to offer access to its own private container fleet through its Premier Service Network, providing a new standard of excellence in intermodal shipping.

*We were not only rewriting the heart of the system for intermodal, we were rewriting it for highway. At the same time, we were introducing an imaging technology and new EDI technology. Then a new financial software package was being transitioned in. I would say that literally 75 percent of the systems that were in place prior to TPS were replaced by the new system. It was a very, very aggressive approach, but it was necessary so that we had one system that would talk to all the other systems. It was a highly integrated approach to the network.*[8]

The new technology would streamline processes so additional hires would not be needed. David Yeager explained, "We looked at ourselves in 2000, and for every million dollars in revenue we made, we needed to add a person with our existing systems. So that was part of our reason for aggressively investing in technology."

In June 2000, David talked to *Crain's Chicago Business* about Hub's technology investment: "Our first priority is to bolster the company's online presence. Our technology spending in 1999 was double the 1998 total and will be higher in 2000." David also declared a priority on increasing Hub's range of services. Logistics revenues doubled in 1998 from the previous year, and increased more than 90 percent in 1999.[9]

Over the next several months, Hub would announce important additions to its IT network.[10] Don Maltby, Jr., who started with Hub in July 1990 as president of the Cleveland operation, began its burgeoning e-commerce division in 1998. He now serves as executive vice president of the logistics division. "E-commerce is how we interface with our vendor community and how we interface with our customer community," Maltby explained. He has overseen the myriad advancements in the division since then.[11]

In September 2000, Hub launched phase two of Hub's online shipment tracking system. Phase two would further ramp up online speed and enhance the ease of use for Hub customers and vendors.[12]

## Hub Announces a Shortfall

Hub's debt load, coupled with its heavy investment in IT and a sluggish economy, eventually took a toll on the company's bottom line. In October, Hub announced that it expected a shortfall in its earnings per share (EPS) estimates for the year 2000's third and fourth quarters. Hub pointed to sharply reduced earnings from the Hub Group Distribution Services (HGDS) subsidiary, and increased costs incurred from creating a new operating system, along with new e-business applications for its core business. The company projected that these additional expenses would pay for themselves by the second quarter of the coming year.[13]

A month after the announcement, Hub initiated a plan to restructure the company's accounting functions by centralizing them at its corporate headquarters in Lombard, Illinois. The plan resulted in the reduction of 56 accounting-related employees from several of the operating companies. Additional cost-cutting measures combined with the centralization of more of Hub's services would continue for another year.

David summed up this challenging period:

*This was a very tough time for us. In addition to an economy that was soft at that point, at the same time we had this massive IT investment for which we*

From Orange County to the Big Apple.

Above: This eye-catching advertisement from 2002 cleverly conveys Hub's expansive networks of offices across the United States.

Left: Bill Crowder, Hub's first CFO, proved instrumental in helping to launch Hub as a public entity.

*were getting none of the productivity gains, and we had 100 percent of the expenses. Added to that, we had interest on our debt, which we were not used to dealing with, nor were we used to dealing with the bankers. Also, our well-liked and well-respected CFO, Bill Crowder, who had helped to take us public, had died of a brain tumor."*[14]

Unbeknownst to David, within a year, all these factors—and more—would contribute to what Mark would later refer to as the perfect storm that would rock Hub to its core.[15]

### Online Advancements

On January 2, 2001, Hub introduced its revamped Web site. The new segment of the site, called Customer Advantage, allowed customers to track shipments, place orders, and obtain pricing online. In regard to the expense involved in this endeavor, Maltby said:

*It's cheaper to transact business on the Web, but to get there, you have to spend a lot of money. We decided we needed to step up our investment in information technology. We decided to invest in the internal structure—how we process orders and how we handle them—and reengineered our entire operating system. At the same time, we invested in developing our e-business strategy.*

Hub's new system wouldn't replace the EDI system favored by the railroads, but it would alleviate what Maltby said was, "the black hole in intermodal that you hear so much about. We've included a function that allows all our draymen around the country to transact their business via the Web. We don't require paperwork unless it's stated on that application for that particular drayage company."[16]

Polsen expanded on the system's new capabilities. "We do a lot of EDI with the rails—hundreds of thousands of transactions on a daily basis. We also use EDI to communicate to our

**HUB EXPEDITED**

Cost-effective, time-saving service that keeps you in control

customers and vendors, but there are a lot of draymen that are very, very small and don't have EDI capabilities. So we created something we call Vendor Interface, which is a Web-based product that was introduced along with TPS. It allows us to tender the freight to the vendors and to the draymen. They can accept the loads that we give them. They can give us status updates for the load, and they can actually also bill using the Web as well."[17]

The rollout of the TPS system would occur in the second quarter of 2001. By then, Hub also expected its new accounting system to be up and running.

This 2002 brochure extols the virtues of Hub Expedited's extensive service network that makes for a smooth, fast, and efficient expedited shipment process.

Previously, individual hubs were responsible for their own billing and collections of invoices, which would now be handled by the corporate office.[18]

At the same time, Hub invested in a network-wide imaging system aimed at reducing the high cost of handling and re-handling shipping documents. The imaging system would allow for the viewing and

Dennis Polsen, current executive vice president of information technology, joined Hub in March 2000 to lead the IT team that would build customized software to integrate the company.

printing of documents using the Internet. Jude Troppoli, a longtime Hub employee, became the director of documentation to oversee the imaging system. He explained:

*In an intermodal move, generally, there are two carriers involved—the carrier that's making the pickup and the carrier that's making the delivery for us. So the bill of lading (a document as evidence of receipt of goods) will be coming from one carrier, and the proof of delivery from the other. With a truck move, also known as a highway move, it's the same carrier, so that bill of lading, which the shipper gives to the driver, in most cases, is the same document that is signed by the receiver when that driver shows up and delivers the freight for us. The imaging system might index 7,000 to 8,000 transactions on an average day. In other words, you'd better have a good documentation system.[19]*

The system would also accurately predict delivery times. "We spend a great deal of time with exception-based tracing," Polsen said. "This is where we have enough history accumulated in the system to be able to accurately predict the rail times associated with every shipment. Along with status reports from the railroads, we can project whether or not the shipment is going to be on time."[20]

In April, Maltby espoused Hub's new online capabilities in a *Chicago Tribune* story, while acknowledging the difficulties involved. "We've invested very heavily in the technology side, all in

all, to redefine our business processes and prepare ourselves for the next 30 years. Our earnings were definitely hit in the year 2000. That's the strategy we decided to take. I think 2001 is going to be a good year for Hub."[21]

On April 19, 2001, Hub marked its 30th anniversary by bringing together its executives for the company's annual three-day gathering. Though the soft economy still negatively affected Hub's bottom line (they had reported fourth-quarter earnings in February of $1.1 million, down from $3.1 million the previous year),[22] the company marked the occasion with a formal portrait that depicts a unified picture of Hub executives, both old and new.

In May, Hub's overseas HLX division experienced a significant loss. The division managed containers for Cho Yang, a South Korean ocean carrier. The arrangement "worked for a while," according to Phil, but Cho Yang abruptly shut down. "We were hung with a large bankruptcy when Cho Yang stopped its business," Phil said. "I'm not trying to criticize steamship companies, but you have to be so careful, and we weren't careful enough. We thought we had a very good situation, but it really nailed us. We'd never had anything like that, but we had to just go through it."[23]

A Korean court rejected the Cho Yang steamship company's application for reorganization and ordered it to liquidate the company. As an unsecured creditor, Hub would not receive any financial remuneration as part of the liquidation.[24] "They tanked us for about $4.7 million," Phil said.[25] This costly occurrence was the critical factor that prompted Hub to announce on September 25 its anticipated shortfall of EPS earnings for the third quarter of 2001.[26]

"We had created HLX in 1994, but it proved to be a very marginal business, with clients that thought paying in 30 days was like cash. Gradually, we lost our desire for the business, especially after the Cho Yang bankruptcy. That $4.7 million loss ruined an otherwise good business year," Phil later commented.[27]

Despite these issues, Hub's reputation in the industry remained stellar. Jim Comerford, vice president of logistics support for Sears Holding Corporation, explained, "The reason why Hub has remained a leader in the field starts with Phil Yeager and then was transmitted to Dave Yeager. Number one, they have integrity and a clear understanding of what drives their business, what it's going to take to be successful. They understand the importance of building relationships not only with the shippers but also with the railroad, because the railroads are the ones that are actually performing the work. And then number two, they have built relationships with the other intermediaries—the drayage and the local distribution areas. It has to start at the top with the commitment to excellence, the integrity, the leadership."[28]

Right: In 2001, Sears Logistics Systems renewed its agreement with Hub for the 10th year in a row, and Sears marked the occasion with a Partners in Progress award for Hub Group.

Below: Hub executives pose for this portrait commemorating Hub's 30th anniversary. Top row, from left: Dick Vara, Mark Young, Dave Porter, John McLaughlin, Tom Juedes, Joe Egertson, Jim Simon, Alan Marks, Don Maltby, Jr. Middle row, from left: Mitch Bernet, Fred Beasley, Vince Anton, Dan Hardman, Greg Smith, Pat Sweeney, Neil Higham, Roger Monaco, Steve Gove. Bottom row, from left: Ed Peterson, Paul DeMerit, Chuck Herzog, David Yeager, Phillip Yeager, Thomas Hardin, Mark Yeager, David Marsh, Tom Reisinger, Jim Gaw.

A bright spot for Hub came in mid-August with the continuation of its strategic alliance with Sears Logistics Services (SLS). The renewed agreement marked the 10th anniversary of the alliance between the two companies. "The success of this evolving logistics alliance, which began as an intermodal process, speaks to the mutual cooperation and efforts extended by both parties. We are extremely pleased to celebrate the 10th year of this important strategic relationship with a major customer," Phil said.[29]

By the end of 2001, the financial fallout from the September 11 tragedy had adversely affected businesses across America, and Hub Group was no exception.[30] Mark said:

*We were going through a pretty dark period. Costs were going up dramatically, the economy and the demand for our services were sluggish, and the competitive environment was fierce. So our margins were contracting at the same time. We were not used to operating with debt. We had always strongly believed in not having any debt, and suddenly we had $150 million worth of debt to deal with. It was a challenge. Kind of the perfect storm, and scary.[31]*

Unfortunately, the perfect storm that had been building over Hub was about to burst forth with a vengeance.

**Stormy Times**

The soft economy hurt Hub in 2001, and revenue decreased 4.6 percent from the prior year to $1.3 billion. Intermodal revenue decreased 9.9 percent from 2000. This resulted from the elimination of Hub's international division. Truckload brokerage had a 2.7 percent rise, and logistics continued to show the biggest growth overall with a 17.8 percent increase in revenue.

As 2002 began, the company suffered as it strove to centralize accounting operations internally, although the investment in Hub's computer network slowly began to pay off.[32] "The margins are always tight in this business, and that's the primary driver behind our investing so aggressively in systems that allow us to be the low-cost option in the long-term in a market that is so competitive," David said about the ongoing IT improvements.[33]

But the improved efficiencies in IT did not find sympathy from the bankers nervously eyeing Hub's debt load. Phil said, "The years 2000, 2001, and 2002 were very difficult for us; we did make a little money, but not enough for the bankers. Bankers love you when you're doing well, but you are 'dog meat' when you can't reduce your debt or meet your financial covenants."[34] Mark said of this period, "There were some tough times when we were running against our debt limits."[35] David put it more bluntly, "These were probably the most difficult years for me personally and professionally. I had made some decisions that were right for the long term, but they shouldn't have all been made at the same time. We breached our covenants six quarters in a row, and that was a nightmare."

David replaced Hub's deceased CFO Bill Crowder, who had helped take the company public in 1996, with another executive. "We were still in the throes of this substantial build, trying to centralize all accounting, which is a huge undertaking. At one point, we had 150 people in finance because we hadn't made the systems right. So these are all the winds that are blowing around," said David.[36]

In February, Hub hired Christopher Kravas, who previously managed his own successful intermodal e-commerce company, Webmodal, acquired by Enron. "Literally the day that Enron filed for bankruptcy on December 3, 2001," Kravas said, "I got a call from Dick Rogan, Hub's head of trucking. He said, 'What are you going to do?' and I said, 'I don't know.' He said, 'Maybe you ought to come here and see if there are some opportunities for us to talk about.' So we met, and that meeting turned into a job."

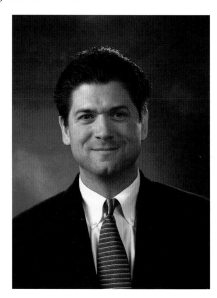

Dick Rogan hired Christopher Kravas (right) in February 2002 to improve operations among Hub Highway's 20 divisions.

Kravas was brought in to act as a liaison among Hub Highway's 20 operating centers and to help streamline operations. "My job was to do everything I could to help those guys grow," he said. "It was a great opportunity to help the company survey what kinds of things were working and not working and to develop some insights into what our key needs were." Many of Kravas' observations would be addressed when Hub would institute company-wide management structure changes a few years later.[37]

HGDS, the company's division that installed point-of-purchase displays, had notified the home office that its largest customer, Phillip Morris, had decided to change its marketing strategy. Mark said, "They were at a point where they really didn't want to emphasize point-of-purchase displays. They didn't feel it was part of their marketing strategy. So they really froze all of that activity, and when they made that shift, our activity got shut down."[38] A significant reduction in Phillip Morris business would adversely affect HGDS's bottom-line expectations. Then Hub would discover another problem with HGDS, thus beginning the company's darkest period.[39]

**Accounting Troubles**

On Valentine's Day 2002, a small story appeared in the business section of the *Chicago Daily Herald* headlined, "Hub Group Finds Accounting Error." The story detailed Hub's announcement two days earlier that it had discovered accounting irregularities in its HGDS division for the years 1999 through 2001. Hub's stock immediately dropped with the announcement. In the words of Phil Yeager, Hub's stock "dropped to a hat size."[40]

Hub owned 65 percent of the division, while its president had a 35 percent ownership stake. Hub did not allege fraud on anyone's part, but pledged to conduct an investigation. The company postponed year-end results until March. Hub estimated the error to be approximately $3.3 million over two years.

During this same period, Arthur Andersen, Hub's accounting firm, was embroiled in the high-profile bankruptcy case involving the energy corporation Enron—for Andersen's questionable accounting practices.[41]

On February 19, investors filed a class-action lawsuit alleging that Hub had misled shareholders over the three-year period of the restatement. The suit claimed that investors "have sustained enormous losses" by relying on the erroneous financial statements.

That same day, Hub announced it had learned that the filings in question violated NASDAQ's rules, and if left uncorrected could subject Hub to delisting. Hub requested a hearing on the matter. The request automatically delayed the delisting process until the hearing could take place, at which time Hub could explain the irregularities. In the meantime, Hub's normal NASDAQ listing of HUBG would change to HUBGE, alerting potential investors that the company was under investigation.

The company moved quickly and aggressively to research the irregularities and rectify the situation. "We are currently doing everything possible with the help of our law firm and a team of forensic accountants to determine the cause of these accounting irregularities," David told *Traffic World* magazine on March 4, 2002. He was quick to note that the irregularities did not involve Hub's core business but rather HGDS's niche logistics division, and that the two maintained separate accounting divisions. David continued, "We have been very aggressive in our communication of the facts, as we knew all too well that one of our less scrupulous competitors would attempt to distribute misinformation. We therefore have communicated directly with our customers and vendors, and intend to continue this effort."

David predicted that Hub would prevail in the class-action lawsuit.[42] Clayton Boyce, *Traffic World*'s editor and publisher, well-versed on the ins and outs of the transportation industry, penned a column in the same issue that overtly supported David's assertion. The editorial, titled "Consider the Source," stated:

*The Hub Group has been hit with a class-action shareholder lawsuit that is nothing but naked opportunism. Is there anyone in the logistics and freight transportation industries who doesn't know Hub Chairman Phil Yeager? Phil has written an annual review of the intermodal industry for*

*Traffic World and has been a notable figure in this business for decades. On the other side is a law firm led by Bill Lerach.* Fortune *magazine called him, "the most loathed and feared lawyer. What makes him loathed is that he is mean: a belligerent, vengeful, foul-mouthed bully," the magazine said in a profile published 18 months ago. The lawyers suing Hub Group can't possibly know of any incriminating internal corporate documents. Their claims are boilerplate accusations that pop up in lawsuit after lawsuit that are nothing more than "greenmail"—shareholder litigation that exploits a sudden drop in a corporation's stock value.*[43]

### Shelter from the Storm

In May, Hub filed documents with the Securities and Exchange Commission (SEC) that detailed the accounting irregularities and notified them that they had replaced Arthur Andersen with Ernst & Young. According to *Traffic World*, "It didn't have anything to do with the restatement. It's just a question of Andersen's health and their ability to service the account. Due to their own financial difficulties, it was obvious that at some point in time, they would not be able to audit public companies."[44]

Hub spent approximately $1 million to go through the process of restating its financial records and putting new procedures in effect. The concerted effort paid off, and the "E" was removed from Hub's NASDAQ listing to notify investors that Hub was no longer under investigation. But the class-action suit remained a concern for Hub. "That we're taking very seriously," Phil said, though he added that he expected the case would be dismissed. On October 23, 2002, the court dismissed the case in Hub's favor.[45] In the midst

of this difficult year, *Traffic World* reported that Hub "was moving slowly but showing progressively more strength."[46]

Next, the company planned to shore up its financial house by bringing in a new CFO who would help to lift Hub out of its financial doldrums.

### White on Board

In 2002, Hub announced that it had appointed Tom White as its new chief financial officer. At the same time, Terri Pizzuto was brought in as vice president of finance.[47] White, who had worked for Arthur Andersen for 23 years, knew nothing about the intermodal industry. But, when approached by David about the position, he realized the job duties would complement his strengths. White recalled, "They had gone public and built a major new technology platform. They had just centralized finance and really needed somebody to help sort it out and get it operating very efficiently. So that sounded like a big challenge. They needed some more help on the banking front with the lenders as well as help on the investor front with the analysts."

White immediately delved in to address these important areas. "It was a time when a lot of companies were having these issues. We weren't the only one. But this was during the Enron bankruptcy, and the whole business community was on edge. I kept looking at the figures and saying, 'That's it?'

Above: Hub's new CFO, Tom White, joined the company in 2002.

Left: Coinciding with Tom White's appointment as CFO, Terri Pizzuto was named vice president of finance. Both are credited with bringing a new financial order to the company's bottom line.

Nowadays, when these restatements occur, you wouldn't even blink at this number. But bankers were all on edge, and we just kind of said to them, 'We'll grant you some more comfort in terms of security, but we need our covenants relaxed so we have time to turn it around.' And they did."[48]

David said, "Tom came in, and he restructured the covenants in such a way that we were going to be able to realistically and continuously meet these commitments. Our previous CFO hadn't done that, because from quarter to quarter he had promised the banks, 'Oh yeah, we'll be better by then.' Well, we weren't."

### Hub Gets Lean

After White examined the financial operations, he came to an onerous conclusion. He approached David with the bad news and said, "You've got to cut." David recalled:

*When Tom came on board, he forged probably some of the most dramatic cultural changes at Hub, because we'd always grown, and you know, growth hides so many warts. All of a sudden we're not growing, and we have a lot of warts showing. He looked at it and said, "You know what? You can't grow your way out of this." Our stock had fallen dramatically, and 90 percent of all stocks that go down to a hat size never get over that, and we were determined to work very hard to turn it around.*

The overall restructuring had taken technology into account, but now Hub found itself with excess staff. David said, "So you begin to look at cutting staff, and ultimately we cut more than 250 people. It's gut-wrenching, especially in the cul-

ture we were brought up in—based on careers, family, relationships. It's just terrible. But I hate to say it, the day after we did it, we looked around and we were functioning. We were overstaffed, and for years, growth had made up for it."[49]

Hub announced this new phase of what it called the long-term improvement plan to the media in October 2002. Hub predicted that by reducing corporate overhead and eliminating obsolete functions deemed unnecessary through the adoption of its new technology, the company would see large financial benefits. As a result, Hub expected $10 million in savings from these actions.

HGDS, which the company had finished purchasing for $4 million in August, would be repositioned to focus on fewer, higher-margin niche services.[50] In addition, Hub's international container repositioning program would also be integrated into its core network to produce greater efficiency. Hub partnered with TMM Logistics to help streamline cross-border shipments to and from Mexico. The Mexico City–based TMM Logistics would provide sales support and operational management in Mexico, with Hub providing the same services in Canada and the United States.[51]

David said, "As a team, we just began chipping away at this, and it's really a credit to the franchise that we survived. I mean, if the franchise was not as strong as it was, we would have crumbled."[52]

Above: In October 2002, Hub partnered with Mexico City–based TMM Logistics to streamline cross-border shipments between the United States and Mexico.

Left: Hub Group offers logistic solutions by providing local access to a network of continent-wide capabilities through its various specialized services.

Hub Chicago President Dan Hardman (now retired) attributed much of the strength of the franchise to its superior executive workforce. "You can't win the Kentucky Derby with a donkey. Hub has more talent. They have better horses."[53]

**The Rumor Mill**

Labor unrest, including work stoppages among draymen, continued to plague the industry in 2002.

In the fall of that year, a dispute with longshoremen shut down all of the West Coast ports for nearly two weeks. A court order reopened the ports under the Taft-Hartley Act, but the shutdown adversely affected Hub's business.[54]

Rumors swirled throughout the industry suggesting that the company was for sale. Several companies even made bids to buy Hub. Hub confirmed the offers in a November 19 press statement where Phil firmly stated, "The proposals that we received for

SUPPLY CHAIN SOLUTIONS

For customized, technology-based logistics programs that reduce transportation costs, turn to Hub's Supply Chain Solutions

the company are not sufficient to support a sale at this time. We firmly believe that Hub Group has great potential as an independent, publicly held entity."[55]

Mark later added, "We had half a dozen offers, all from U.S. sources that understandably wanted to buy us on the cheap because we were going through a rough time."[56] Throughout these difficult times, Hub's hierarchy strategically mapped out a plan to put Hub back on track.

### The Big Idea

Mark recalled the circumstances that sparked the idea that would rejuvenate Hub. "We had really struggled to try to implement strategy and make it work across the interests of all the hubs, and that was a challenge. Everything we did we had to try to find a way to make it advantageous for all of those profit and loss statements (each operating company had its own), and it was very frustrating."

One afternoon, heading to the airport for a business trip, Mark had a conversation with John Healy, Hub's vice president for supply chain solutions at the time. Mark recalled:

*We were talking about how difficult it was to get things done at Hub, and how long it took, and how you had to really try to work hard to create buy-in. John said to me, "What if you didn't have the P&Ls? What if Hub looked like a regular company?" I couldn't even fathom it. That was beyond my comprehension, because this was the world I had grown up in.*

*But it remained in the back of my mind. I just kept thinking about it, and when I had a free moment, I'd try to visualize what that company would look like. What is this thing? How does this work? How is this structured? How do we not have 28 different, separate P&Ls?*

*Eventually, I started making notes and diagramming. Then one day, I shared the idea with Tom White and Chris Kravas. I said, "Let me show you something that's just been bouncing around in my head a little bit." I put the diagram up on the board.*

White and Kravas, both experienced with companies that did not have separate P&L statement business models, immediately saw the feasibility of Mark's idea. The trio spent several days further developing it. Mark continued, "Basically, we were slotting everybody and visualizing how the organization would look, how we would build it, and how we would compensate people."

After formalizing the concept, Mark, White, and Kravas presented the idea to Hub CEO David Yeager for consideration. Mark recalled, "His first reaction was that this went to the very fabric of the organization. That was the idea."[57] White said, "Dave sent us back to the drawing board to make some revisions. He said, 'You've got to cover this, this, and this before you sit down with Phil,' which is what we ultimately did."[58]

With David's support, a small team would be formed to develop a concrete management-restructuring plan.[59] Gaw, who joined Hub in 1988 as a territorial sales manager and later became president of the company's upper Midwest operation, recalled:

*I was based in Milwaukee, and I remember the exact day that Mark started talking to me about the change. He called me the week before Thanksgiving in 2002 and said, "Hey, do you have any time to come down to Chicago next week?" and I said, "Sure." I came down and had lunch with him the day before Thanksgiving, and we sat in his office. Mark had the structure drawn up on his whiteboard, and he said, "What do you think of that?" I looked at it, and I said, "Wow. That structure is a very traditional structure for most organizations. For Hub, it would be revolutionary." Mark said, "Well, just think about it, and we'll get back together as a group. We'll put a team together, and we'll start talking through it in the new year."[60]*

As 2002 concluded, Hub had survived its own perfect storm, and charted a course in a positive direction that would permanently alter and improve its management structure. Though the industry

Opposite: Hub touted its ability to deliver supply chain solutions in this brochure from 2003. Hub provides expertise in driving cost savings and enhancing efficiencies to create customized solutions to improve supply chain performance for its customers.

and the stock analysts did not yet know it, the dark period for Hub had come to an end.

### The Turnaround

Hub Group, Inc., started off 2003 by moving its headquarters to Downers Grove, within eyesight of its old space in Lombard, Illinois. The office occupied two floors of a traditional glass-and-chrome building in a quiet, tree-shaded office park, off a winding road. The reception area featured tasteful displays of many of the Hub honors received from its high-profile retail clients including Home Depot, Target, and Sears. The all-important IT systems, critical to Hub's service efficiency in the age of

Above: Hub Group, Inc., moved its corporate offices to this modern office building in Downers Grove, Illinois, 10 miles west of Chicago in January 2003.

Right: Hub received many recognitions for its outstanding service, including the 2001 Shipper of the Year award from long-time Hub business partner BNSF Railroad, the 2002 Excellent Supplier award from intermodal partner TTX, and the 2003 Intermodal Carrier of the Year award from retail giant Target.

computer technology, are housed elsewhere for security reasons.

At the beginning of 2003, plans for the company's restructuring, called the realignment, began to take shape. Gaw said, "In February 2003, a team was put together, and we started working on the transition plan in earnest. We began with putting the structure together and deciding who would be fulfilling various roles. We worked on that for a good part of that year. I spent a lot of time in Chicago that year working on that and doing my job up in Milwaukee, too."[61] White recalled:

*Mark Yeager was really the visionary there. Mark was really the leader. Chris Kravas was also a big part of this. We got together, and we looked at it for about a year, and studied alternative structures. Ultimately, we got the Hay Group involved, which is a compensation benefits consultant group, and really spent a lot of time on putting people in the roles that would best suit their strengths. As opposed to everybody being a generalist, we kind of said, "Let's focus people on intermodal or truck or highway or logistics." Then, to Dave Yeager's credit, he said, "I want to give everybody skin in the game." So about 105 people were offered restricted stock in the company. I think the stock was down in*

*the teens or thereabouts. So, by offering restricted stock two or three layers down, it gave employees some ownership.*[62]

But that financial incentive would come after formulating and executing the plan. The plan involved dramatically altering the management structure of Hub once and for all. Hardman, president of Hub Chicago, said:

*We didn't really have uniform practices through-out the organization. We simply bought out the owners. A couple of them left; the other guys put their money in the bank and stayed, and nothing really changed, as far as the practices. Not until we changed the structure with the realignment, where there would be no more operating companies. The Hub Operating Company structure stayed there after going public. We tried, but I don't think we were real successful in changing to common company practices. So we decided to eliminate the operating company structure. Period.*

The realignment would completely change the overall structure of the company. Hardman explained, "The biggest stumbling block was that in each office there was a guy, and he set the tone. The guy at the top always sets the tone, no matter what it is—good, bad, or indifferent. So you had somebody at each office that still had the title of president, even though he was no longer an owner.

In the past, that person set the agenda for everybody involved in the operation. So that role would be eliminated with this new structure, and everything would be uniform."[63]

Ongoing discussions regarding the new business model continued for months. Gaw said, "You know, you're sitting around and you're looking at various options, and who can do what, and that sort of thing. There was a point where it became clear that it was going to happen."[64]

With the strategy in place, the real challenge now involved convincing Phil to agree to the entire realignment plan. White said, "I think the big event in all of this was when we prepared everything ourselves to sit down with Phil Yeager and convince him that this made sense. That was probably the hardest part of the whole project. We put together PowerPoint presentations, and really, it was Chris Kravas and Mark Yeager who led it. If Phil's stamp of approval wasn't on it, it wasn't going to happen. He had built the company, and it was a dramatic change. Getting his blessing was critical."[65]

Above left: A rare glimpse at Hub's off-sight computer operations critical to Hub's efficient and effective customer service offerings.

Above right: Mark Yeager, Hub's president since 2003, envisioned and championed the company's corporate restructuring effort.

Right: James Gaw served on the team that actively participated in the planning stages of the company's restructuring strategy.

"It was a long time in coming," Phil said, "And probably because of the history of the company and the fact that we had been so successful for that extended period—for almost 30 years—I probably fought it. David pushed it. He was the guy that drove it home."[66] Mark said, "When Dave and I took it to my father, he was concerned about the implications for the organization. But as he thought about it, he recognized that we needed to make a change, that we needed to become a network, that we needed to stop fighting each other, and this new plan had the potential to do that."[67] Hardin said:

> You can imagine Phil's and my reaction to that, after all these great years of success with our team. "Whoa … what are you doing here?" But, the more we got into it, the more the light bulb went on. This makes a lot of sense if we're going to grow, and we're going to become a better company.[68]

Both executives had learned to trust their instincts and take risks. It had been a hallmark of Hub's success. "I think when we got our backs up during this period where we said, 'Hey, we've been laying around here. We're not moving. We are not doing things.' This was a way to do that," Phil said. "I think when Tom White came in, we started to understand how to do some of these things because he had the financial knowledge that we'd been missing."[69]

Dan Hardman, Hub Chicago president, recognized the value of the management restructuring plan, which would strengthen the organization and sharpen its competitive edge.

With some convincing, Phil signed off on the new realignment. White said, "Once we knew that Phil supported it, we knew it was going to work."[70]

**The Realignment Unveiling**

With Phil's approval, the idea for the management restructuring moved to the next level. Mark said, "We made the group a little bit bigger. We brought in the people who we saw heading up these various functional units, the guys who we thought of as executive vice presidents (EVPs) and who, under our plan, ultimately became EVPs, the guys that would lead the business units. We rolled it out to them. Over the course of about 16 months, we put this thing together, and finalized it, and got it ready."[71]

"Along August or September of that year, it started to sink in that this was going to happen," Gaw recalled. "We managed to keep it really quiet up until the announcement date. It was a really small group that had knowledge of it. People were starting to ask some questions about what all these meetings were about. The rumor mill was that we were being sold. It was an interesting time at Hub. It was really exciting and scary at the same time."[72]

After making key executives aware of the restructuring, Hub planned to announce its new realignment strategy to the media in early December. Before doing so, however, a serendipitous event occurred that would sweeten the announcement.

**Hub's Stock Rebounds**

"In 2003, we started to come back into our own," Phil said. "The analysts had all dropped us. So we didn't have anybody watching us as we started coming up. By the fourth quarter in 2003, we were ripping and roaring, and they still hadn't realized it."[73]

White said, "No one was interested in Hub on the street. They had dropped us, because as far as they were concerned, we had become an uninteresting story. That was part of the agenda: Get our debt situation taken care of, get the cost structure down, and get the operating efficiencies wrung out of the business, because we have invested so heavily in information technology. Then it was time to get some coverage on the street."[74]

On December 5, Gary Yablon, a leading stock analyst with Credit Suisse First Boston, recognized Hub's revitalized potential. "We see Hub in the early stages of a significant turnaround in the non-asset based intermodal marketing business. Hub Group is both cost and revenue driven, which should allow the company to regain a degree of intermodal share lost in the 2000 to 2002 time frame." He gave Hub an outperform rating and a 12-month target price of $30 per share. Hub's stock price jumped more than 10 percent with the announcement.[75] "It jumped that day because he had such a good following," White said. "I'll never forget driving to work that day."[76]

Then five days later, on December 10, Hub announced its realignment plan. A front-page story in *Traffic World* trumpeted "Realigning Intermodal: Hub Group Ditches Franchise Model for 'Network' Approach to Win Back Business." The story revealed that the new management plan would go into effect in February 2004, and also carried the news of the stock coverage. The new single network business model would markedly enhance Hub's position in the industry. "We're prepared to grow," Phil said.[77]

After the most difficult period in the company's history, Hub's extraordinary comeback was just beginning.

In March 2006, NASDAQ recognized Hub for its 10-year anniversary as a publicly held company with this bold announcement.

# CHAPTER EIGHT

# BACK ON TRACK

## 2004 AND BEYOND

*Today the railroads realize they need us more than ever before.*

—Phillip Yeager

HUB GROUP BECAME galvanized by the upturn in its stock after investors noted the company's turnaround—a turnaround that occurred because of Hub's stringent cost-cutting measures and its customer service enhancements resulting from its major investment in technology. Hub expected to see even greater revitalization due to its corporate restructuring that would commence on February 1, 2004.

As the year began, the railroad service failures that had mostly faded within the last three years had returned to plague the industry in certain heavy-traffic areas during peak shipping periods. Phillip Yeager remained optimistic on the state of the railroad industry in a January 2004 supplement to the *Journal of Commerce*, "We do not believe the railroads have approached maximum capacity and believe this problem will be resolved as we enter 2004." Phil also predicted that rivalries for business in the extremely competitive intermodal industry would only heighten as other IMCs ramped up their technology systems and trucking companies increased their intermodal usage.[1]

Hub Group had diversified its services to the point where intermodal accounted for 75 percent of its business, trucking for 15 percent, and logistics for 10 percent. The impending company restructuring plan would serve to increase its share in both its trucking and logistics businesses.[2]

Hub's new corporate structure would change the company from a business with individual profit and loss centers at each of its operating centers, to a single, unified company with decision making in sales, intermodal, highway, and logistics coming from the corporate headquarters.

Centralized pricing for containers and better management of equipment supplies at peak seasons was the easy part of Hub's aggressive restructuring plan. Implementing the internal aspects would prove a greater challenge. Stephen Cosgrove, Hub's executive vice president of intermodal operations and administration, explained:

*The biggest problem was to be able to have each of the offices do everything across the board really well. To excel in all of the service areas was really hard. Based on the guy that ran that particular office, whatever his natural skill was, whether he was a great sales guy, a great logistics mind, a highway guy, or an intermodal oper-*

This oil painting, which depicts Hub's bright red containers traversing a scenic mountain pass, graces Hub's executive suite at the company's headquarters in Downers Grove, Illinois. *(Painting by David J. Tutwiler OPA)*

*ations guy, that was the strength of that office, and that office took on the characteristic of that leader. So, we had offices that were extremely good in highway, but their intermodal operation was really bad, and the intermodal operation was only as strong as its weakest link. So it was our task to make the other offices as strong as the Chicago office. To replicate all of the intermodal operation offices, get them as similar and as cost-efficient as possible.*[3]

One regional office might specialize in logistics or excel in sales, depending on the experience of its president. But the restructuring was intended to develop expertise across the board in all regions for each of Hub's business lines. David Marsh, Hub's executive vice president of highway, said, "Highway was probably underinvested before the realignment. So there were a lot of offices that may not have had highway expertise from a management perspective. At the time, people who had intermodal experience were hired because that was the core of the company's business at that time. As we evolved, that meant fewer of the management folks had highway experience. With the restructuring, we would have folks focusing on managing people in all the areas."[4]

In order to get each hub operation up to speed, the company initiated new management training programs. Cosgrove explained, "You develop a list of operational metrics of things that you want every office to be able to do. You set goals for them, and you meet with them on a regular basis, and check to see how they're doing against their metrics. You show them ways to improve their processes." The majority of the division leaders were brought into Chicago and trained in running a business in a team atmosphere.[5]

James Gaw, executive vice president of sales, described another change that would occur as a result of the realignment, "Traditionally, there were many instances where a salesperson virtually owned the entire relationship with a customer. It wasn't always a Hub relationship. So we worked hard not to take that relationship away, but to expand upon it, and to get other people involved to ensure that it was also a Hub relationship."

The company hierarchy recognized a need to revamp Hub's incentive plan as part of the reorganization. Gaw explained, "One of the things that we did was redesign the sales compensation programs. There were 45 different plans through the organization, which was messy. So we boiled them down to basically three plans. Under the new plans, in order to be successful, each operation needed to see its revenues grow. That was not the case in most of the previous compensation plans. Margin was the driver—not a bad thing—but here they would have an incentive to develop new business and to expand old business. Our goal is to grow, obviously, and in order to align the various hubs with that concept, we had to have an incentive that focused on growth."[6]

To streamline operations and reduce business redundancies, the realignment would call for staffing changes, including reducing the sales force from 130 to 90 employees.[7] Job responsibilities would change for about 15 percent of the company's employees—most of whom were previous hub presidents.[8] Mark Yeager commented:

*You could roll something like this out, and it could fail miserably if you didn't have all the i's dotted and the t's crossed, and all the questions answered. We tried to do that thoughtfully and compassionately. We knew the employees' strengths, and we knew their weaknesses, and that was the key. So we drafted the best players for the right positions. A certain individual might have been stronger in an operations role, and we drafted him for an operational position. We knew them all, and we went through the players and spent a lot of time on that. Most of them were extremely pleased with the result. They'd say, "You're right. I'd really like to sell. That's what I want to do." Or, "I really am stronger in operations." I think that was the key to the success of the realignment.*[9]

**Making it Work**

The realignment kickoff occurred on February 1, 2004. Gaw said, "On that first day, David Yeager held two all-company video conferences. Dave did a really great job of not just describing what it was going to be like but also assuring people that their lives weren't going to change significantly. Once people heard that, they felt pretty good about it."[10]

# HUB'S STRATEGIC PLAN

IN THE EVER-CHANGING ENVIRONMENT of freight transportation, what strategy should an industry leader like Hub Group follow to maintain its prominence and guarantee future growth? Evolution is the key, according to Hub's CEO, David Yeager, who conveyed the importance of adaptation as the cornerstone to Hub's success. "Like all industries, transportation is evolving, and as the industry has grown up, our thoughts have also evolved—and will continue to do so."

In its early days, Hub placed an emphasis on optimizing each and every transaction. David commented:

*When my dad started the company, optimizing every transaction was the way to make money in the intermodal business. It has evolved to be much more of a network play because many of the asset players have come into the business. The way that they look at the world was different from just on a per-transaction basis. The biggest change you see is the asset providers are basically changing the rules of the game to a large extent, and we've been one of the few IMCs that have been able to adapt to those changes.*

In the short range, the trends that are currently impacting the industry in a positive way include a truck driver shortage, high fuel prices, and the rise of international trade. Hub can provide lower costs to its customers through rail freight transportation, which generally has a significant fuel efficiency advantage over trucking.

In addition, David expects international trade to continue to benefit Hub for the fore-seeable future. "We see no sign that this is going to change, and that's driving a lot of the dynamics of the intermodal business. Again, the goods are traveling a longer length of haul in this country because many of them are coming in from the Far East."

By becoming an asset-light provider, Hub Group has focused on another key strategy. David explained, "When you become a network provider and you're moving your own assets, you do begin to look at freight flows, at balance, at turn times. There's a whole set of different issues, and we're more focused on getting good business and not just any business."

Local drayage also remains a key ingredient in the mix. David explained:

*We spend $300 million a year in local trucking. We still need to outsource. Even today, our Quality Service and Comtrak divisions only represent 30 percent of our overall local drayage business. We see that as an area that we need to get more efficient at and expand in. We can deliver better customer service and reduce costs through further development of our own drayage capabilities. We will, of course, also continue to utilize outside drayage companies to help support our business.*

Finally, the strategy for growth at Hub Group will remain the same as the day Phillip and Joyce Yeager first opened up for business. David said, "What we're really trying to do is focus on our core business and how to do that better. We're focusing on our core transportation products and enhancing those, and getting them bigger and better."[1]

Ten days later during a transportation conference, David discussed the positive effect he expected the realignment would have on the company:

*We feel as though this simplified structure is going to give us a tremendous amount of advantages. Number one, we believe that it will drive sales growth. We now have one salesperson who all of our salespeople report to. So there's one focus, one agenda, driving business to where we want it and when we want it. We believe that this is going to have a very powerful impact on the overall organization. Our plan for the future is top-line revenue growth first and foremost. We believe that the realigned structure, coupled with the information technology we have invested in, poised us very much for growth. And, if you look at the models—if, for example, we anticipate a 1 percent top-line growth, our earnings per share increase by about 10 cents. So there's a lot of power, a lot of leverage there that's available to us to generate this top-line growth. In addition, we're not going to forget cost controls. We are very focused on that. We have ongoing measures that will allow us to continue to become a leaner, more competitive company.*

*In addition, margin enhancements are an ongoing effort, and they range the gamut from accessorial processes to looking at our bottom 40 accounts from a gross margin perspective and looking for ways to enhance the margin on those accounts. Last but not least, is network optimization. Since we've gone public eight years ago, the intermodal business has changed dramatically. It is not a business where you can focus solely on transactions. You have to operate as a network in order to be competitive, and we believe that this realignment positions us for that.*[11]

Internally, the changes received a positive response from the outset. Brian Avery, Hub's senior vice president of intermodal, said, "I think it probably exceeded expectations by a long shot. It went really well. Maybe it's luck, and maybe it's skill, but it seemed like all of the moves and reassignments were very obvious and made a lot of sense. The right people got put in the right slots. I think some of that might be coincidental; some of it might be because of the way the new organization was structured. It certainly exceeded my expectations."[12]

**The Pay Off**

By April 2004, the results of Hub's corporate realignment, which dramatically lowered costs across the board, were already positively affecting the company's bottom line. In addition, an unforeseen factor contributed to Hub's financial health. The large-scale movement of U.S. manufacturing and jobs overseas by retail giants like Target, Home Depot, and Sears would increase Hub's management of freight shipments for these and other retailers. "A lot of the products being manufactured in China now are coming through the West Coast," David said in an April 12, 2004, *Crain's Chicago Business* article. "At certain times, it's tough to find enough containers and trailers for shipping all these goods."

This 2005 advertisement boasts Hub's acquisition of 3,400 new containers to its fleet, and it guarantees equipment availability to its customers through the industry's first equipment guarantee program.

The article noted that Hub's management restructuring would improve coordination throughout the organization, serving as a key component in claiming more business from new customers. Investment analyst Alexander Brand commented, "Hub has turned its operations around by focusing on the cost side of the equation. The next phase is to go out and win more new business."[13]

A month later, in May 2004, *Traffic World* reported a remarkable accomplishment for the company: Record first-quarter profits that directly followed the corporate restructuring. Hub earned a net profit of $2.7 million for the quarter ending March 31, nearly double the previous year's net profit of $1.4 million. Though revenue slipped, costs and expenses were also down. David said, "We are delighted with the improvement in our profitability. During the remainder of the year, our management team will continue to focus on leveraging our new structure to drive revenue growth, improve operating efficiency, and enhance customer service."

During the first quarter of 2004, Hub also paid down $5 million of debt and modified the debt agreement with its bank group to secure lower interest rates, giving the company some much-needed breathing room.[14] Tom White said, "We got a lot of efficiencies out of our new structure. This is what is supposed to happen when you go through this kind of transformation. You go public. You invest. You get your cost structure under control. We changed our sales force compensation plan. The efficiencies have led to a head count reduction. There was a whole team that made this happen. Certainly a key person in the whole Hub financial transformation is Terri Pizzuto, the vice president of finance."[15]

Hardin identified another factor resulting in the success of the realignment, "I think that, because we were so in step and involved with the folks in the field, our restructuring went more smoothly than a normal corporate restructuring would where no one is a real name or face. They're a number. In this case, we had compassion, and we knew these fellows."[16]

Mike McClellan, vice president of intermodal and automotive marketing for Norfolk Southern Railroad, one of Hub's longest standing rail partners, said about Hub's realignment:

Hub's business success hit the headlines of the *Chicago Sun-Times* in October 2005, when the newspaper reported on the little-publicly-known-but-incredibly-successful Hub Group. In the article, CEO David Yeager discussed the intricacies of the business operation.

*It's probably one of the most important and profound changes I've seen an intermodal company make in my tenure in this business.*

*Why has Hub been able to persevere? I'd go back to the innovation side. Sometimes they lead the innovation, and sometimes they follow, but they've always had enough creative talent and innovative talent to ensure their success.*[17]

Mark, the strategist behind the realignment, became a director of the company and chief operating officer in May 2004, due in great part to his vision of Hub as a network-based company.[18]

### Freedom from Debt

Hub had survived the financial challenges of the previous two years. It experienced a dramatic comeback resulting from its network-based company restructuring and its heavy investment in information technology. But the company was still weighed down by $50 million in debt. Phil said, "That time period was really difficult for us. But we had that large debt to contend with. When we went public in '96, we had zero debt. Zero debt! I hate debt more than anything."[19]

After Hub's stock made a dramatic upswing with a price of $33 per share, the company announced a stock offering to help pay off its debt. The offering of 1.8 million shares of Class A common stock, was made on July 2, 2004.[20] The offering netted the company close to $56 million—enough to prepay the debt and most of the prepayment penalty.[21] Phil said, "It was a drain on us, and we really worked through it, and that's what I'm so proud of."[22]

### Recognition and Awards

*American Shipper* magazine profiled Phil with an in-depth story in its September 2004 issue. The article covered Phil's inspiring personal and business history.[23]

Around the same time, Target Corporation had, for the second year in a row, named Hub Group their Intermodal Carrier of the Year. In presenting the award, Target cited Hub's great efforts in improving its transportation and administrative initiatives on behalf of the retailer.

Target also singled out Hub's importance as a participant in numerous administrative projects for Target, including helping to simplify its EDI and freight payment functions. Also, Hub's ability to increase equipment capacity during peak shipping seasons contributed to earning the award for a second year in a row. Finally, Target recognized Hub Group's "intangible values such as industry knowledge, preventing potential service disruptions, and excellent relationships with the nation's railroads, and other aspects related to the intermodal industry, all of which were a benefit to Target."[24]

David said, "We are very pleased to be recognized as a leading service provider by Target Corporation. Receiving this recognition by a major client like Target is a satisfying reflection of Hub's ongoing dedication to provide our customers with the highest quality of intermodal management services that enable increased cost savings and a greater degree of customer satisfaction."

Hill's, the global leader in pet nutrition, presented Hub with its Intermodal Carrier of the Year award in 2004 for Hub's dedication to customer service.

John Bauer, senior manager of domestic transportation of Target said, "They understand the markets. I consider Dave Yeager a friend, and I think he's been real forthright in terms of this partnership. If we're not their largest shipper, we're close to it, and he's really been a good partner. The good companies tend to be good at relationships, and I think even from a financial perspective. And the companies that struggle with the relationship side of the business tend to struggle with their financials, too. Hub has been willing to take some very significant risks with us and I think, in turn, we have been able to go out on the limb for them, too. I think that in itself is the definition of a partnership."[25]

In November 2004, The Home Depot also selected Hub for its Intermodal Partner of the Year award. The Home Depot recognized Hub for exceeding expectations by "improving service levels, proactively solving rail and drayage issues, and providing excellent administrative assistance." David said, "Being named Intermodal Partner of the Year by The Home Depot is a great honor for our company. Receiving this award is validation of Hub's commitment to providing our customers with the most cost-efficient, highest-quality intermodal management services. We greatly appreciate the recognition."

Commenting on The Home Depot's successful business relationship with Hub, Maria Ross, director of transportation for the retail giant, explained:

*Hub Group has taken the time to understand our business needs and has developed models to fit the needs of The Home Depot. Hub Group understands the challenges within the supply chain as well as with servicing a retail consumer and has developed solutions that best fit the needs of our customers. Hub Group prides itself on providing a high level of customer service. Hub takes the time to understand the needs of its customers and adjust its service levels to meet the demands of the business. Its management team proactively works with our team, anticipating challenges and developing contingency plans to mitigate potential risk. Through the senior leadership at Hub Group and The Home Depot, we have grown the business in less than one year 50 percent.*[26]

### A Record End to a Record Year

In addition to receiving recognition from its biggest clients, Hub Group reached another milestone

As The Home Depot's 2004 Intermodal Partner of the Year, Hub Group received recognition for its ongoing commitment to providing its customers with high-quality, cost-efficient intermodal transportation services.

when it announced second-quarter profits in the fall of 2004. Hub's net income from January through June showed a 133 percent increase over the same period in the year before. Furthermore, from January to June, the stock price jumped 60 percent. Lower overhead and the corporate restructuring contributed to Hub's impressive net income.[27]

In November, Hub entered into a purchase option and right of first refusal agreement with William J. McKenna for the purchase of HUB Group Distribution Services (HGDS). McKenna, then-president of HGDS, agreed to a purchase option of more than $11 million for the division. He also promised to stay and run the division at least until November 2007.[28] Mark explained the reason for the sale:

*What HGDS does is a good business; it can be a profitable business, and it has been for us. However, it really has very little connection to our core business. The business involves installing display racks, and that has almost no connection to what we do on the highway side or the logistics side, and certainly not on the intermodal side. Also, because it's project work, it tends to be very lumpy. It can have very robust quarters and very slow quarters. It just no longer fit into the Hub business model.*[29]

December 2004 brought more good news to the company. *Forbes* magazine recognized Hub Group as one of the 400 best big companies in the country for the year. Companies were selected based on value-added corporate practices as well as positive revenue flow.[30] Then, later that month, *CBS Market Watch* reported that Hub's stock earned an important upgrade by the stock analyst company Bear Stearns from peer perform to outperform. Bear Stearns analyst Edward Wolfe forecasted a stock increase to $70 a share by the end of 2005. "We believe there remains at least as much upside potential. And, after spending an increased amount of time with Hub Group management over the past nine months, we firmly believe in the story and the management team," Wolfe said. "We believe all the pieces are in place for Hub Group to continue the evolution from a 'good to great' company and for shareholders to benefit along the ride."[31]

The year 2005 would bring Hub even more financial rewards and recognitions, along with a challenge from the intermodal industry that would once again heat up the competition.

### Passing the Baton

Hub Group began 2005 with an announcement. On January 1, Mark Yeager, chief operating officer, received the appointment of president—taking over the helm from Hardin, who had held the post since 1985. Hardin was named president of rail affairs.[32] "The appointment of Mark Yeager as president will help Hub better execute its sales strategy and improve network operations," Phil told the press in making the announcement. About Hardin's new post, Phil said, "One of Tom Hardin's major roles with Hub Group over the years has been to maintain a close working relationship with the railroads. In his new capacity, Tom will be able to devote full time to the important ongoing strategic negotiations required to ensure Hub Group always has the required service options and equipment available for its customers—especially during this time of tight capacity."[33]

Hardin later reflected on Mark's appointment, "I think I planned for that when he was 12 years old. I feel like I am almost a family member. I probably am as close to Dave, Mark, and Phil as I am with my own family. We grew up together over 30 years. So this was a natural event that we all had talked about. The time came when it was the right step. I think we really worked closely the prior year on a lot of the nuances of the job. I helped to groom him, although he didn't need a lot of that because he grew up in the business.

In 2005, The Home Depot presented Hub Group with this keepsake when Hub again earned the retail giant's designation of Intermodal Partner of the Year.

# MORE THAN INTERMODAL

AN IMPORTANT ASPECT OF HUB GROUP'S continued success involves strategic diversification. But diversification doesn't mean straying far from Hub's proven areas of expertise. Mark Yeager, Hub's president and chief operating officer, commented, "We're not talking about making massive leaps in terms of diversification; we're not going into fundamentally different types of businesses. We're not going to go into the business of selling copiers or anything like that. Our diversification is really the product of logical extensions of what we can do for our customers."

For Hub Group, diversification involves a continuous expansion beyond its core business of intermodal. Mark said:

*Ten years ago, we were 95 percent intermodal. We're 73 percent intermodal now. We really have branched our services out to not only offer highway and logistic solutions but also to be in aspects of the intermodal business that we were not in previously—specifically drayage. We've expanded our control of the dray process and our engage-*

*ment in the dray process. That's something we will continue to expand moving forward. I also see that both logistics and highway have great growth opportunities. So I think the trend from 95 percent of one type of service offering to 75 percent will continue. Near-term, we'll be 50 percent intermodal and 50 percent other services.*

*We certainly want to find a way to participate more actively in the international side of the industry. All the research indicates that international business will continue to see high single- and double-digit growth, and we need to find a way to be more actively engaged in this side of the business.*

Hub faces some challenges as the company strives to further diversify. Mark explained, "People tend to think of us as solely an intermodal company. So it's important to educate our shippers about the variety of services we can offer them. Also, as a company, we tend to have an intermodal mindset. We need to be able to look at a variety of solutions that we can provide to our customers—not just an intermodal one."[1]

So this wasn't anything overnight. This was in the making for quite a while."[34]

Mark discussed Hardin's contributions to the company:

*Tom has done such a terrific job for our organization, and he's really led the company in so many ways. He is absolutely a legend in our industry. People within the rail industry, in particular, have tremendous respect for Tom. He's one of the brightest people and one of the most street-smart people you could ever meet. On top of that, he is a great, great negotiator and continues to really help our company deal with our partners in a way that nobody else could. He's a person that really has always put the company first. I've known him since I was about eight years old, so it's an amazing thing. It's a real treat to be able to work with someone that you've*

*known that long, and that has done such a great service for the company, and for my family. I have tremendous respect for him. After all these years, I don't think of Tom as a co-worker, I think of him as a member of the family.*[35]

Mark and Hardin assumed their new responsibilities as Hub continued to experience a dramatic financial resurgence. It reported $7 million in profit for the fourth quarter of 2004—a record over the previous year by a remarkable 164 percent. Hub's revenue for the quarter was up 7.9 percent to $387.4 million. During this financially vibrant period, Hub authorized a $30 million stock repurchase plan. Hub announced that it would seek shareholder approval to increase Class A common shares for a two-for-one stock split at its shareholders' meeting in May.[36]

A model of an 18 wheeler with Hub's traditonal blazing red container bearing the recognizable Hub Group logo.

More good news came in March when *Fortune* magazine named Hub Group as one of the nation's most admired companies for 2004. To compile the list, *Fortune* magazine solicited input from top executives and analysts who rated top companies within their particular industry. The respondents were also asked to rank the top 10 companies across all industries, and Hub Group made that prestigious all-star list.[37]

### Hub's Evolving Strategy

David reflected on Hub's outstanding comeback at the Deutsche Bank Securities Transportation Conference on February 16. He said, "Highlights of 2004 would include converting our business model successfully. The numbers will show that. The new business model enabled us to focus on each significant business segment within our company. The result of that is a strengthened brokerage and logistics business, which really manifested itself in the fourth quarter."

Next, Mark shared a preview of the year ahead for Hub:

*From an intermodal perspective, we really have four central themes for 2005. The first is capacity: 2004 saw an unprecedented tightness of capacity throughout the country, and we think that that's a trend that's going to continue into this year and probably beyond. There's also, obviously, a significant concentration on preserving our margins, as third-party margins are relatively tight, and it's very important that there be a lot of focus on margin preservation. Drayage control is another significant issue. Much like intermodal equipment, intermodal drayage is very tight in many markets, and driver recruitment is an extremely difficult issue to deal with. We're taking steps to help alleviate this problem. Finally, growth—profitable growth being the caveat there.[38]*

### Hub Acquires Its Own Containers

To help manage the equipment shortages, Mark explained, "We are purchasing 3,400 fleet boxes that are 53 feet long, which we'll be plugging into our overall capacity. We'll have all our boxes within our fleet in time for peak season at the end of July. From a sales perspective, we're giving our salesmen something to sell in the form of additional capacity. We need to do everything we can to develop that capacity, and we believe that with improved operating disciplines, improved sales disciplines, and improved pricing disciplines, we will produce profitable growth."[39]

Hub purchased the new bright red containers emblazoned with the distinctive Hub Group logo in white from Shanghai Jindo Container Company, a subsidiary of South Korean–based Jindo Corporation, at a cost of approximately $33 million.[40]

Aside from providing Hub with a competitive edge in controlling capacity, the decision to acquire the containers was also in response to BNSF Chairman Matt Rose's vision to substantially reduce its trailer and container fleet. This decision would allow the railroad to eliminate the high costs associated with managing these assets. The announcement was of no surprise to long-time observers of the transportation industry. "We saw this trend of asset ownership coming, we just thought it would come faster," Phil said. "Yes, it has become part of the business." The new

containers would require storage facilities, and, after eight years into its Premier Service Network program, Hub already had its own depots in traffic-heavy markets such as Chicago, Los Angeles, and Atlanta. "We're able to keep our finger on the equipment and keep turning it," Phil said.[41]

Mark described how Hub would transform itself to maintain its relationship with BNSF:

*BNSF is a vendor that has an economic model that says, "I really like people to bring their own assets." So our choice was to not do business with the highest service railroad in the United States or change our model and bring some assets to the table. It helps us have a long-term seat at the table with a very highly valued vendor, in a relationship that brings value for both parties. They like it, and we like it. It's a change for us, always having been non-asset based, but it's positive.[42]*

Hardin echoed this sentiment and explained the concept in more detail, "It's changed the course for Hub, because it puts us into a really unique situation. We're so different from the other IMCs, who rely totally on railroad equipment. It puts us into the model of the asset-based profitability econom-

Hub purchased 3,400 of its own fleet containers in an unprecedented strategic move to control its own capacity and harness an advantage over its competitors.

# HUB'S BIG RED BOXES

WHEN HUB GROUP ORDERED ITS own containers—all 3,400 of them—in spring 2005, it intended to maintain its competitive edge by overcoming equipment shortages through the management of its own fleet.

The boxes, which can weight up to 57,000 pounds when filled, were manufactured in Shanghai, China. While shipping the boxes overseas, the barge encountered rough weather and 46 of the containers, at the estimated total cost of more than $400,000, went overboard into the ocean.[1] James Gaw, executive vice president of sales commented, "We weren't liable for that, but who knows? Maybe we have an artificial Hub reef somewhere out there in the Pacific."[2]

In order to receive approval by the Association of American Railroads (AAR), a prototype container requires rigorous testing. Brian Avery, the company's senior vice president of intermodal, traveled to China to oversee testing of Hub's new containers. According to Avery:

*You load the container to twice its weight-bearing capacity, lift it up, and measure the deflection of things. In this test, you simulate the container being dropped. Then you straddle-lift it. Basically, what you try to do is to break it, and you try to twist it corner to corner. Then you push the top. You simulate some very, very rigorous handling and riding on a train during its life.*

*Next, you set it down and make sure it goes back to the way it was. Then you put big airbags in it and try to blow*

*the nose and the back doors and the sides out of it. Then you load it with an irregularly placed load, very heavy in the middle, and lift that up. You test the roof for strength. You test it for watertightness. You simulate 3,000 forklifts' movements in and out of it, and you simulate lifting it and setting it down 1,500 times. Obviously, those last two tests take quite a while—several days to complete, in fact.*

A well-maintained container can last decades, though most are replaced within 10 to 12 years. Avery said, "It's like a car: You can keep it repaired, but eventually you tire of it. As a result of the wear and tear, after containers get to a certain age, they

become a marketing liability, because of their appearance and things like that. They have serviceable life, but they also have a marketing life."[3]

Hub's big red boxes are designed to high standards to ensure they can transport the myriad products demanded by Hub's wide array of clients. And because the containers—unlike boxcars—spend relatively little time sitting at depots or in train yards, they are less susceptible to vandalism. "However, there is some very sophisticated cargo theft that goes on. We've had instances where people actually never broke the seal and emptied a complete container," Mark said. "They popped the door off the hinges—and these are massive doors. They take those off, empty the container and then put them back on. When they go by inspection, the container is sealed, and nobody has any idea they've been emptied." Of course, these are rare occurrences. In fact, Hub maintains one of the lowest loss ratios in the industry.

An important factor regarding containers involves product consistency. "Our boxes are consistent with what else is out there in the marketplace, because consistency is a virtue when it comes to containers. They have to be durable enough so you can afford to keep them repaired, but they also have to be light enough so that you can load a competitive weight. Customers count on that consistency," Mark explained.[4]

In May 2005, Hub received the first shipment of its new brightly colored containers, changing Hub from a non-asset- to a light-asset-based company.

ics, without having the balance sheet issues. It allows us to capitalize on our good railroad relations. It also allows us to remain neutral because we're not 'all in' on one railroad. In other words, we can do our asset thing on BN and NS, but we can also do business with UP, CSX, and Pacer, and they like that model. So we're in the middle. It's a great strategy." The model has proven so successful that Hub has recently extended its asset management strategy with Union Pacific for private equipment.[43]

David described some additional advantages regarding the container purchase, "With the new containers, we can additionally handle approximately 100,000 loads, which will help with the tight capacity within intermodal. From a sales perspective, we really haven't grown our top line as much as we would like over the last five years. The added capacity is going to give us the ability to handle that business. In the intermodal business, you'd usually expect to see a peak in the third and fourth quarter. That did not occur for us in 2004. That's because we're at capacity, using all the boxes that are available. Our increase in boxes will help rectify that situation."[44]

### Unyson Logistics

In late March 2005, Hub announced a new designation for its logistics division—Unyson Logistics. "We chose to rename our logistics operation for several reasons," Mark said. "A primary objective was to more clearly delineate our logistics products and services from those of the other divisions within Hub Group—intermodal and highway services. It's a highly specialized discipline, and the re-branding effort will give our logistics expertise a more focused presence in the marketplace."[45]

Don Maltby, Jr., executive vice president of Unyson Logistics said, "Another key reason for this re-branding is to bring to the forefront the core promise we make to our customers every day. In fact, we've put that cornerstone value right in our name. 'Unyson' stands for working collaboratively, in union with our customers, to create the best possible customized solution for elevating supply chain performance."[46]

Also in March, for the third year in a row, Hub Group gained recognition in *Fortune* magazine by appearing on its list of most admired companies for 2005.[47]

Additionally, *Traffic World* reported that Hub Group had again posted record earnings. Net income for the quarter ending March 31, 2005, reached $5.3 million, 97 percent higher than the first quarter of 2004. Revenue grew by 3.5 percent to $339.9 million as compared to $328.3 million in the first quarter of 2004.[48]

### A Successful Summer

Hub's cost-cutting measures realigned operations and helped to improve its margins, and now Hub focused on winning over business through signed contracts to help it boost its market share. Hub had already doubled its Home Depot revenue from $17 to $34 million over the previous year. Bear Stearns analyst Ed Wolfe noted in a June 22, 2005, *Traffic World* article, "We believe there remains tremendous upside over the next 12 to 24 months for Hub, provided it can accelerate its revenue growth, which we believe is very likely given visibility to intermodal trends, its improving operations and sales effort, and recent customer wins."[49]

Hub's exceptional fiscal performance continued when the company reported record second-quarter earnings. For the quarter ending June 30, 2005, Hub's net income reached a record $7.9 million, a 95 percent increase in second-quarter net income over the 2004 figure. Hub's revenue grew by 6.5 percent to $371.6 million, as compared to $349 million in the second-quarter of 2004. Second-quarter intermodal revenue increased 4.6 percent to $259.3 million. Truckload brokerage revenue increased 19.8 percent to $68 million this quarter. Second-quarter logistics revenue increased 2.2 percent to $34.5 million.[50] Regarding the overall positive results David said, "We are pleased with our record second quarter. Our focus on yield management, while maintaining effective control of our costs, continues to generate strong shareholder returns." At the same time, Hub's board of directors approved a two-for-one stock split in the form of a stock dividend, which was paid out on May 11, 2005.[51]

Hub's financial improvement continued into the fall of 2005. In October, it announced that third-quarter profits almost tripled to $9.6 million from $3.6 million in the same period the previous year. Revenue grew to $399 million, as compared to $362 million in the third quarter of 2004, an impressive increase.

Hub's business success was well known within the transportation industry, but mainstream America knew little, if anything, of Hub's existence. But in October, the *Chicago Sun-Times* would change all that. The newspaper featured Hub Group in what the newspaper defined as its "occasional series of the least discovered major companies in Chicago." The story profiled the pioneering intermodal company and noted that Hub was well on its way to achieving a record of almost $1.5 billion in revenue for the year.

The story also discussed that, ironically, the current outsourcing trend that sent jobs and manufacturing overseas in record numbers, served as a boon to the intermodal industry. In the arti-

Hub CEO David Yeager envisions Hub Group's continued success by focusing on its core competencies and planning for strategic growth.

cle, David said, "Bringing in all those foreign-made goods, and shipping ours to markets abroad, has vastly lengthened the average shipping distance today. So many products must start or finish at seaports, and the longer the distance to ship, the more competitive our railroads are, in many cases a full 30 percent less expensive than cross-country trucking."[52]

Left: Comtrak Owner and President Mike Bruns sold his multi-million dollar company to Hub Group in 2006. Retained by Hub as part of the sales agreement, Bruns manages the Comtrak division along with Hub's Quality Service branches.

Below: Located on 39 acres in Memphis, Tennessee, Comtrak's corporate headquarters houses all of its administration, information systems, and customer service employees.

Utilizing Hub Group provided advantages beyond cost savings. David explained, "Take a client like the Hussman Division of Ingersoll Rand, a leading producer of huge refrigerators for supermarkets. They send us the order electronically, we study the matrix of transportation, routing and timing options, and plan the optimal mode to have those products sent to the designated customer with speed and efficiency. To do this, we've invested $60 million in consolidating all of our control systems into one control complex at our Downers Grove headquarters, staffed by 57 information technology specialists. The operation tracks the location and status of each unit we have in transit, every minute of the day."[53]

Though Hub Group had a great 2005, the rest of the intermodal transportation industry didn't necessarily follow suit. In Phil's annual January column for the *Journal of Commerce,* in which he discussed industry trends, he said, "Any review of 2005 must begin with the sharp increase in cost that rocked our industry throughout the year. It's painfully obvious that this has been primarily driven by fuel. Compounding this cost problem, our industry continues to face ongoing service and capacity issues."

Phil said that he expected these problems, which the industry had surmounted in the past, would ease in the year ahead. But the 2005 shift in rail attitude toward non-asset-based companies wasn't about to change anytime soon. Phil commented, "Some in the rail industry now place more weight on asset ownership than proven performance. This shift, when combined with poor rail service, has forced smaller IMCs out of the intermodal industry. Not all the railroads are following this policy, and I believe there is still room for the IMC. Railroads may change their minds again on this issue."[54]

**Hub Acquires Comtrak**

On January 30, 2006, *Traffic World* reported on Hub Group's intended purchase of Comtrak, a Memphis, Tennessee–based trucking company. Through the purchase of this company at the price of $48 million, Hub Group would increase its presence in drayage markets as well as gain access to drayage technology developed by Comtrak. "We

have worked with Comtrak for 20 years and believe this is the best drayage company in the country," David said in making the announcement. "This acquisition makes Hub a stronger company and a more formidable competitor."

The company provides truckload transportation, container storage, yard management, and truck brokerage. Its 381 employees and 15 terminals (most in the southeastern states) would vastly increase Hub's drayage network. The company assets included 250 tractors and 650 trailers. Comtrak's revenues in 2005 were estimated at about $85 million. As part of the sales agreement, Hub would retain Mike Bruns, who established Comtrak in 1983, to continue to run Comtrak, as well as taking over the management of Hub's Quality Service branches.[55]

David Zeilstra, Hub's vice president and general counsel commented, "Mike Bruns is very respected

An artful memento created in recognition of Hub's purchase of Comtrak trucking on February 28, 2006.

# HUB: PAST, PRESENT, AND FUTURE

REFLECTING ON HUB GROUP'S HISTORY, Phillip Yeager said, "When we started in 1971, we were strictly an intermodal company. We weren't called intermodal marketing companies then—we were called shipper agents. At that time, our industry was very disreputable, but our company worked hard to change people's attitude toward the intermodal marketing company—as we were called starting in the 1980s."

During the industry's initial stages, the field was crowded with what Phil referred to as fast-buck guys.

*They didn't know anything about intermodal. But, today, the intermodal marketing companies that are well run, like ours, have a place in the future of the industry. Intermodal has tremendous promise. People are starting to understand and realize that the railroad is the way to go with long-haul freight because it's more economical, and*

*when the service is good, it's a wonderful way to ship freight. It costs less and it can be very attractive to large companies that have high volume.*

Upgrades to the current rail system (an investment projected to cost upward of $50 billion by 2010) will further benefit Hub. "I think this segment will be our largest and most profitable business in the future," Phil said.

Capacity will also be an important element to future growth for Hub and other IMCs. Though Hub has 13,601 containers in its fleet, Phil said, "We are looking at expanding that fleet."

But Hub isn't just about intermodalism. Hub Highway Services, launched in 1996, is now one of the largest truck brokerage operations in the United States. With more than 10,000 carriers under contract and an enviable customer list, Highway Services is the fastest-growing division of Hub Group, posting a 13 percent compound annual growth rate over the past three years.

in the industry and very respected by each of the Yeagers. There was a long-term relationship between the two, so it's one of those deals that both sides felt very good about. There's a lot of trust. When we were looking for somebody, Comtrak was at the top of the list."[56]

Bruns explained the reasons why Hub was the right fit for his company:

*Within the first 20 loads that we hauled when I started Comtrak in Memphis in 1983 with three tractors, there were loads for Hub City in Memphis. We have an old dispatch sheet hanging in the hallway—the first one—and there are plenty of Hub City entries on it. So my relationship with Hub dates back to July 1983 through this period right now. They were a great company to do business with and certainly recognized as a leader in the field, and I'd like to think we were kind of a leader in our field. Smaller niche, but certainly a good fit. I had known them for 20 years, and if you're going to get married, I would rather get married to someone whom I've been dating for 20 years, than someone I just met. Their integrity is impeccable. Their handshakes are gold, and that just makes you want to do business with them. They also had opportunities for me with their own truck line that I could help them improve, make it bigger and better, and combining it with ours would give my people some opportunities to do things they always wanted to do. When you put all that in a pot and shake it up, you've got a deal.*[57]

Comtrak's presence in the international drayage market served as a key factor in making the deal. "Instead of buying an international freight forwarder in China, this makes a lot of sense for us to be able to enter that market," David said. "Comtrak has relationships with steamship lines, but what we bring to the table are tremendous relationships with some of the largest big-box retailers and other large importers that can decide how to route various shipments."[58]

David Beasley, Hub's vice president of drayage management, expanded on the acquisition of Comtrak, "This is getting Hub into a different arena. It's going to automatically open up doors for us to start handling some import containers, which gives us an opportunity to reload them back to the ports. Our Quality Service fleet is about 500 trucks, and Comtrak has about the same, so the acquisition basically doubled our fleet overnight."[59]

Steve Rand, an executive with CSX Intermodal, and longtime Hub supporter, commented about what he called Hub's strategic and creative acquisition of Comtrak. "It really lends itself to a creative type of solution where Hub's going out and controlling the drayage capacity. So now when they talk to their national accounts and their big customers, they've got a leg up because not only do they have favorable contracts with railroads but they now control the end-to-end door deliveries. That's going to really create a winning proposition for them in the marketplace."[60]

George Baima, executive vice president of Pacella Trucking Express and longtime friend of both Bruns' and the Yeagers', said about the deal,

---

Logistics, a relatively new aspect of intermodal marketing companies, will continue as a growth profit center for Hub. Phil said, "We're still relatively new in it, but it's growing, And again, we're getting better at it. I think this industry has tremendous potential," Phil said.

Hub will also experience growth in the international arena. Phil, who gives speeches on the intermodal industry in America and abroad, finds that the industry is gaining acceptance globally.

Hub Group's recent purchase of Comtrak targets the international market. "Comtrak is very, very large in the drayage part of the international business," Phil commented. "The potential for growth is very large."

In a final assessment of Hub's extraordinary history and future, Phil commented:

*I'm amazed. I really feel that we are just getting started. We've been in business 35 years, but the rapid changes that are occurring in the industry and in transportation as a whole are just so great that it's mind-boggling. It is good that we have a young management team who has a great deal of experience and is doing a wonderful job of taking us into the future.*[1]

Posing in full academic regalia, Phil Yeager graciously accepted his honorary doctorate degree from the University of Denver on June 9, 2006.

"The marriage is going to be great. Mike Bruns is a great individual. He and I are very, very close, and I go way back with the Yeagers. This is going to be a really good marriage."[61]

Hub's purchase of Comtrak would have an immediate effect on the company's trucking presence across its network, as Jim Ronchetto, Hub's president of Quality Services noted, "The Comtrak acquisition put us in 15 additional cities overnight. Probably the only area of the country that we're not in today would be the Pacific Northwest, the Seattle-Portland area, and the East Coast. If it makes sense to go into those additional cities, we'll go there."[62]

### Asset Light

Less than a month after the Comtrak acquisition, Hub again reported record profits. For the fourth quarter of 2005, profits had risen a notable 45 percent to $10.1 million, compared to $7 million in the fourth quarter of 2004. The company credited strong demand for its services, and increased rates as key factors for the increase. David said, "Over the last several years, we've seen very aggressive pricing by the rail carriers, as tight capacity has given them the power to increase rates at historic levels. When we get an increase, we pass it on, but I don't think as 2006 unfolds that the same level of increase is pending. Right now, a little breathing room is appropriate."

Revenue for Hub grew to $420.6 million for the quarter, an 8.6 percent increase over the previous year. David said that Hub anticipated a strong year ahead despite industry-wide predictions of a flat year for the rest of the domestic intermodal industry.

David said, "International business has certainly been the growth engine with all the overseas manufacturing that's going on, and we see that growing another 7 to 8 percent. On the domestic side, I think all railroads recognize they want to be in the market."[63]

Hub's fourth-quarter intermodal revenue increased 11.8 percent to $302.3 million, truckload brokerage revenue increased 15.6 percent to $71.2 million, and HGDS' revenue increased to $17.4 million. Logistics had a slight decrease in revenue to $29.7 million. For 2005 overall, revenue hit $1.5 billion, a 7.3 percent increase over 2004, with net income increasing 53.2 percent to an impressive $32.9 million.[64]

With the release of these figures, and the finalization of the Comtrak deal, Hub Group, Inc., after almost 35 years in business as a non-asset-based company, now proclaimed itself as an "asset-light management company."[65]

"Our company had been non-asset focused forever. In fact, it was a big reason why drayage was not considered an option for a long time—because we just did not want to own assets," said Joe Egertson, vice president of Unyson Logistics. "We made an awful lot of money without owning assets and without taking on that liability and risk. Fortunately, our leadership team saw the changing landscape and reacted faster than anybody else did. They got into business with BNSF, and it changed the landscape. You had the haves and the have-nots, and the have-nots are the majority of the players in the intermodal marketing arena."[66]

Mike Carrol, Hub Seattle director of intermodal operations concurred. "Hub is pretty good at looking in the crystal ball and seeing what's coming, and what we are going to do to accommodate it. Our fleet was a very good example of that. There were a lot of growing pains with it at first, but it turned out to be one of the most brilliant decisions of all, because as time has gone on, the amount of available equipment has declined almost constantly. With the Hub Group fleet in place, we are very well positioned.[67]

### Hub Celebrates 35 Years

As spring 2006 was ushered in, Hub had much to celebrate. *Fortune* magazine's April issue had once again singled out Hub for inclusion on its Fortune 500 list.[68] Also in April, the University of Denver announced that it would award Phil an honorary Doctor of Public Service degree for his important contributions to the creation and growth of the intermodal transportation industry.

Later that month, Hub announced its first-quarter earnings for 2006. Breaking its own record again, Hub reported income for the period ending March 31, 2006, of $8.5 million, an increase of 80 percent over first-quarter income from the previous year. The results included the first month of operations for the Comtrak acquisition. Hub's revenue grew by 8.3 percent to $356.7 million, compared to $329.4 million in the first quarter of 2005. First-quarter intermodal revenue increased 11.3 percent to $260.7 million, which included the addition of Comtrak. Truckload brokerage revenue increased 16.4 percent to $69.5 million, and first-quarter logistics revenue experienced a 25.3 percent loss down to $26.5 million.

Hub would officially divest itself from its HGDS division in the next 60 days, and therefore, the company discontinued reporting financial results for this division. David said, "We are very pleased with the quarter. The divestiture of our HGDS installation business furthers our strategy of focusing on our core transportation business, and our acquisition of Comtrak strengthens our intermodal franchise."[69]

Coincidentally, the Hub earnings report was made on April 19, 2006—the same day as the company's 35th anniversary. "We sent out a big birthday cake to each of the hubs," Phil said. "In the old days, I encouraged all the hubs to do that for each birthday. We also sent a birthday cake to the folks who work in the yards. It went over really great. Everyone sent us some kind of reply—we got notes, faxes, phone calls, e-mails. It went over big. Old-timers really got a kick out of it. People really appreciate things like that. That's what Hub has been all about."[70]

### The Legend Continues

As Hub executive Cosgrove noted, "The future is for the nimble,"[71] and for 35 years, that has been just one hallmark of Hub's success. But certainly, other factors contributed to the enormous growth and prosperity of the company—factors like vision, hard work, integrity, and dedication. All of these attributes can be found in the example set by Phillip and Joyce Yeager, when they started their business—in a one-room, windowless office the size of an elevator, with a single desk—and saw their tiny company grow into a billion-dollar-plus corporation with more than 1,000 employees. As Mark noted, "I think it's a great American success story."[72]

In reflecting back on his business achievements, Phil said:

*The thing that I'm the most proud of is the people in our company—and we have had a lot of wonderful people. We've been very fortunate, and we see a great future. The new challenges we face are things that we can do as well, or better than, our competition, and we're going to do them. We're going to continue to satisfy our customers.[73]*

# Notes to Sources

**Chapter One**

1. Robert Mottley, "Intermodal Logistics," *American Shipper*, September 2004.
2. Phillip Yeager, interview by Jeffrey L. Rodengen, digital recording, 1 September 2005, Write Stuff Enterprises, Inc.
3. Ibid.
4. Ibid.
5. "Intermodal Logistics."
6. Ibid.
7. Phillip Yeager, interview by Jeffrey L. Rodengen.
8. "History of Bellevue," www.bellevue.org/history.htm/.
9. "History of Cincinnati," http://www.cincinnati.org/.
10. Phillip Yeager, interview by Ann Gossy, digital recording, 9 November 2005, Write Stuff Enterprises, Inc.
11. Phillip Yeager, interview by Jeffrey L. Rodengen.
12. Phillip Yeager, interview by Ann Gossy.
13. Phillip Yeager, interview by Jeffrey L. Rodengen.
14. Ibid.
15. Ibid.
16. Ibid.
17. Ibid
18. Ibid.
19. Ibid.
20. Ibid.
21. Christopher T. Baer, "A General Chronology of the Pennsylvania Railroad Company," http://www.prrths.com/PRR_hagley_intro.htm/.
22. Phillip Yeager, interview by Jeffrey L. Rodengen.
23. Ibid.
24. "Intermodal Logistics."
25. Ibid.
26. Phillip Yeager, interview by Jeffrey L. Rodengen.
27. Ibid.
28. Ibid.
29. Ibid.
30. Ibid.
31. Ibid.

**Chapter Two**

1. "Hinsdale History and Architecture," http://www.villageofhinsdale.org/history/history.php/.
2. "History of the Graue Mill and Museum," http://www.grauemill.org/history.htm/.
3. Phillip Yeager, interview by Ann Gossy, digital recording, 5 December 2005, Write Stuff Enterprises, Inc.
4. Phillip Yeager, interview by Jeffrey L. Rodengen, digital recording, 1

September 2005, Write Stuff Enterprises, Inc.

5. Ibid.

6. Ibid.

7. Ibid.

8. Ibid.

9. Ibid.

10. Ibid.

11. Debra Jensen, interview by Jeffrey L. Rodengen, digital recording, 10 November 2005, Write Stuff Enterprises, Inc.

12. Phillip Yeager, interview by Jeffrey L. Rodengen.

13. Ibid.

14. Ibid.

15. Thomas Hardin, interview by Jeffrey L. Rodengen, digital recording, 1 September 2005, Write Stuff Enterprises, Inc.

16. Phillip Yeager, interview by Jeffrey L. Rodengen.

17. Anne Schmitt, "Hub Group's Growth Has Been on Fast Track," *Daily Herald*, 8 May 1996.

18. Phillip Yeager, interview by Jeffrey L. Rodengen.

19. Ibid.

20. Ibid.

21. Thomas Hardin, interview.

22. Phillip Yeager, interview by Jeffrey L. Rodengen.

23. Phillip Yeager, interview by Ann Gossy.

24. "Hub Group's Growth Has Been on Fast Track."

25. "Intermodal Logistics."

26. Phillip Yeager, interview by Jeffrey L. Rodengen.

27. Ibid.

28. Thomas Hardin, interview.

29. Phillip Yeager, interview by Jeffrey L. Rodengen.

30. Thomas Hardin, interview.

31. Phillip Yeager, interview by Jeffrey L. Rodengen.

32. Thomas Hardin, interview.

33. Phillip Yeager, interview by Jeffrey L. Rodengen.

34. Thomas Hardin, interview.

35. Phillip Yeager, interview by Jeffrey L. Rodengen.

36. Thomas Hardin, interview.

37. Ibid.

38. Phillip Yeager, interview by Jeffrey L. Rodengen.

39. Ron Hazlett, interview by Jeffrey L. Rodengen, digital recording, 3 October 2005, Write Stuff Enterprises, Inc.

40. Ibid.

41. George Olson, interview by Jeffrey L. Rodengen, digital recording, 30 May 2006, Write Stuff Enterprises, Inc.

42. Ibid.

43. Thomas Hardin, interview.

44. Phillip Yeager, interview by Ann Gossy.

45. Phillip Yeager, interview by Jeffrey L. Rodengen.

46. Thomas Hardin, interview.

47. George Woodward, interview by Jeffrey L. Rodengen, digital recording, 15 June 2006, Write Stuff Enterprises, Inc.

48. David Yeager, interview by Jeffrey L. Rodengen, digital recording, 1 September 2005, Write Stuff Enterprises, Inc.

49. Mark Yeager, interview by Jeffrey L. Rodengen, digital recording, 31 August 2005, Write Stuff Enterprises, Inc.

50. John T. Slania, "Yeager Puts Transportation Company on the Fast Track," *Alumni News/Class Notes*, Winter 2000.

**Chapter Two Sidebar: Chicago: The Crossroads of America**

1. John C. Hudson, "Railroads," Encyclopedia of Chicago, http://www. encyclopedia. chicagohistory.org/.

**Chapter Two Sidebar: Nabisco and Hub: A Lasting Relationship**

1. Donald Maltby, Sr., interview by Jeffrey L. Rodengen, digital recording, 6 December 2005, Write Stuff Enterprises, Inc.

**Chapter Two Sidebar: "Ship-a-Train" Takes Off**

1. Thomas Hardin, interview by Ann Gossy, digital recording, 14 December 2005, Write Stuff Enterprises, Inc.
2. Phillip Yeager, Presentation from the Intermodal Founding Fathers of North America Conference, 27–29 July 1999.
3. Ibid.
4. Ibid.
5. Ibid.
6. Thomas Hardin, interview.

**Chapter Three**

1. Phillip Yeager, interview by Jeffrey L. Rodengen, digital recording, 1 September 2005, Write Stuff Enterprises, Inc.
2. Robert Mottley, "Intermodal Logistics,"

*American Shipper,* September 2004.
3. "Finance Encyclopedia," http://www.finance-encyclopedia.com/term/subchapters/.
4. Thomas Hardin, interview by Jeffrey L. Rodengen, digital recording, 1 September 2005, Write Stuff Enterprises, Inc.
5. Phillip Yeager, interview by Carolyn Quayle, Oral History Interview transcript, the Intermodal Founding Fathers of North America Conference, 28 July 1999.
6. Phillip Yeager, Presentation from the Intermodal Founding Fathers of North America Conference, 27–29 July 1999.
7. Phillip Yeager, interview by Jeffrey L. Rodengen.
8. Thomas Hardin, interview.
9. Phillip Yeager, interview by Jeffrey L.Rodengen.
10. Ibid.
11. Ron Hazlett, interview by Jeffrey L. Rodengen, digital recording, 3 October 2005, Write Stuff Enterprises, Inc.
12. Ibid.
13. Thomas Hardin, interview.

14. David Yeager, interview by Jeffrey L. Rodengen, digital recording, 1 September 2005, Write Stuff Enterprises, Inc.
15. Ibid.
16. Chris Merrill, interview by Jeffrey L. Rodengen, digital recording, 27 January 2006, Write Stuff Enterprises, Inc.
17. Ed Peterson, interview by Jeffrey L. Rodengen, digital recording, 9 June 2006, Write Stuff Enterprises, Inc.
18. Ibid.
19. Ibid.
20. Robert Jensen, interview by Jeffrey L. Rodengen, digital recording, 5 December 2005, Write Stuff Enterprises, Inc.
21. Debra Jensen, interview by Jeffrey L. Rodengen, digital recording, 10 November 2005, Write Stuff Enterprises, Inc.
22. Thomas Hardin, interview.
23. Tom Holzmann, interview by Jeffrey L. Rodengen, digital recording, 6 December 2005, Write Stuff Enterprises, Inc.
24. Thomas Hardin, interview.

25. William Schmidt, interview by Jeffrey L. Rodengen, digital recording, 11 October 2005, Write Stuff Enterprises, Inc.
26. Ibid.
27. Ibid.
28. "Harley Orrin Staggers," http://en.wikipedia.org/wiki/Harley_Staggers/.
29. Ibid.
30. "Impact of the Staggers Rail Act of 1980," www.fra.dot.gov/downloads/policy/staggers_rail_act_impact.pdf/.
31. "H.R. 4570," Library of Congress, http://thomas.loc.gov/.
32. "Staggers Rail and Motor Carrier Acts of 1980," *Bookrags Business Study Guide*, http://www.bookrags.com/other/business/staggers/.
33. Presentation from the Intermodal Founding Fathers of North America Conference.
34. "Intermodal Logistics."
35. Maralee Volchko, written correspondence via e-mail, 14 October 2005.
36. Thomas Hardin, interview.
37. Jim Klingberg, interview by Jeffrey L. Rodengen, digital recording, 13

April 2006, Write Stuff Enterprises, Inc.
38. Phillip Yeager, interview by Jeffrey L. Rodengen.
39. Ibid.
40. Joe Wallace, written responses to interview questions by Jeffrey L. Rodengen, via e-mail, October 2005.
41. Ibid.
42. Phillip Yeager, interview by Jeffrey L. Rodengen.
43. Jim Decker, interview by Jeffrey L. Rodengen, digital recording, 4 April 2006, Write Stuff Enterprises, Inc.
44. Ibid.
45. Maralee Volchko, written correspondence.
46. Phillip Yeager, interview by Jeffrey L. Rodengen.
47. David Yeager, interview.
48. Ibid.
49. Phillip Yeager, interview by Jeffrey L. Rodengen.

**Chapter Three Sidebar:
Ron Hazlett**

1. Phillip Yeager, written correspondence to Ann Gossy, 22 December 2006.

**Chapter Three Sidebar:
Hub and the Railroads:
Parallel Tracks**

1. Phillip Yeager, written correspondence to Ann

Gossy, 22 December 2006.

**Chapter Three Sidebar:
The Making of a Hub**

1. Phillip Yeager, written correspondence to Ann Gossy, 22 December 2006.

**Chapter Three Sidebar:
The Innovative Double-Stack**

1. "Union Pacific Company Overview," http://www.uprr.com/aboutup/history/uprr-chr.shtml/.
2. "Intermodal Freight," http://www.wikipedia.org/wiki/Intermodal_freight_transport+history+of+the+doublestack+container/.
3. "APL History," http://www.apl.com/history/topics/innovate/rail.htm/.
4. Michael Blaszak, "Intermodal Equipment," *Trains*, 11 September 2002.
5. "APL History," http://www.apl.com/history/topics/innovate/rail.htm/.
6. Ibid.
7. Phillip Yeager, interview by Carolyn Quayle, Oral History Interview

transcript, the Intermodal Founding Fathers of North America Conference, 28 July 1999.

**Chapter Four**

1. David Yeager, interview by Jeffrey L. Rodengen, digital recording, 1 September 2005, Write Stuff Enterprises, Inc.
2. Phillip Yeager, interview by Carolyn Quayle, Oral History Interview transcript, the Intermodal Founding Fathers of North America Conference, 28 July 1999.
3. Ibid.
4. Maralee Volchko, written correspondence via e-mail, 14 October 2005.
5. David Yeager, interview.
6. Phillip Yeager, interview by Ann Gossy, recording, 16 January 2006, Write Stuff Enterprises, Inc.
7. Thomas Hardin, interview by Jeffrey L. Rodengen, digital recording, 1 September 2005, Write Stuff Enterprises, Inc.
8. Ibid.
9. Tom Reisinger, interview by Jeffrey L. Rodengen, digital recording, 26 September 2005, Write Stuff Enterprises, Inc.
10. Phillip Yeager, interview by Ann Gossy.
11. Phillip Yeager, interview by Carolyn Quayle.
12. Phillip Yeager, interview by Ann Gossy.
13. Joseph Bonney, "Phillip Yeager's Hub Group," *American Shipper*, May 1991.
14. John Donnell, interview by Jeffrey L. Rodengen, digital recording, 28 September 2005, Write Stuff Enterprises, Inc.
15. Ibid.
16. Maralee Volchko, written correspondence.
17. Tom Reisinger, interview.
18. Joe Wallace, interview by Jeffrey L. Rodengen, digital recording, 12 October 2005, Write Stuff Enterprises, Inc.
19. Maralee Volchko, written correspondence.
20. Donald Maltby, Sr., interview by Jeffrey L. Rodengen, digital recording, 6 December 2005, Write Stuff Enterprises, Inc.
21. Donald Maltby, Jr., interview by Jeffrey L. Rodengen, digital recording, 31 August 2005, Write Stuff Enterprises, Inc.
22. Ibid.
23. Mike Blackwell, interview by Jeffrey L. Rodengen, digital recording, 6 March 2006, Write Stuff Enterprises, Inc.
24. Phillip Yeager, Presentation from the Intermodal Founding Fathers of North America Conference, 27–29 July 1999.
25. Joseph Bonney, "Phillip Yeager's Hub Group," *American Shipper*, May 1991.
26. Phillip Yeager, interview by Ann Gossy.
27. Ibid.
28. Thomas Hardin, interview by Ann Gossy, digital recording, 15 February 2006, Write Stuff Enterprises, Inc.
29. "Phillip Yeager's Hub Group."
30. Phillip Yeager, interview by Carolyn Quayle.
31. Mark Yeager, interview by Jeffrey L. Rodengen, digital recording, 31 August 2005, Write Stuff Enterprises, Inc.
32. "For Rail Intermodal, Santa Fe and J. B. Hunt Plan a Quantum Jump. (Quantum Rail-Truck Joint-Service

Agreement)," *Railway Age*, January 1990.

33. James Gaw, interview by Jeffrey L. Rodengen, digital recording, 1 September 2005, Write Stuff Enterprises, Inc.

34. Tom Holzmann, interview by Ann Gossy, digital recording, 13 February 2006, Write Stuff Enterprises, Inc.

35. Phillip Yeager, interview by Ann Gossy.

36. Ibid.

37. Donald Maltby, Jr., interview.

38. Phillip Yeager, interview by Ann Gossy.

39. "Form 10-K," Hub Group, Inc., 22 March 2002.

40. Phillip Yeager, interview by Ann Gossy.

**Chapter Four Sidebar: What Is Drayage?**

1. Phillip Yeager, written correspondence to Ann Gossy, 22 December 2006.

**Chapter Five**

1. "Present at the Revolution," Q&A Captains of Industry Feature, *Logistics Management*, November 1997.

2. David Yeager, interview by Jeffrey L. Rodengen, digital recording, 1 September 2005, Write Stuff Enterprises, Inc.

3. Phillip Yeager, interview by Carolyn Quayle, Oral History Interview transcript, the Intermodal Founding Fathers of North America Conference, 28 July 1999.

4. "Form 10-K," Hub Group, Inc., 22 March 2002.

5. Phillip Yeager, interview by Carolyn Quayle.

6. Ibid.

7. Mark Yeager, interview by Jeffrey L. Rodengen, digital recording, 31 August 2005, Write Stuff Enterprises, Inc.

8. Phillip Yeager, interview interview by Carolyn Quayle.

9. "W. Edwards Deming," http://en.wikipedia.org/wiki/W._Edwards_Deming/.

10. Mark Yeager, interview.

11. Ibid.

12. Phillip Yeager, interview by Jeffrey L. Rodengen, digital recording, 1 September 2005, Write Stuff Enterprises, Inc.

13. Thomas Hardin, interview by Jeffrey L. Rodengen, digital recording, 15 February 2006, Write Stuff Enterprises, Inc.

14. Harry Inda, interview by Jeffrey L. Rodengen, digital recording, 11 October 2005, Write Stuff Enterprises, Inc.

15. Thomas Hardin, interview.

16. Tom Reisinger, interview by Jeffrey L. Rodengen, digital recording, 26 September 2005, Write Stuff Enterprises, Inc.

17. Ibid.

18. Dick Rogan, interview by Jeffrey L. Rodengen, digital recording, 27 January 2006, Write Stuff Enterprises, Inc.

19. Ibid.

20. Phillip Yeager, written correspondence to Ann Gossy, 22 December 2006.

21. "North American Free Trade Agreement," http://en.wikipedia.org/wiki/North_American_Free_Trade_Agreement/.

22. Tom Holzmann, interview by Ann Gossy, digital recording, 13 February 2006, Write Stuff Enterprises, Inc.

23. Thomas Hardin, interview.

24. David Yeager, interview.

25. Phillip Yeager, interview by Jeffrey Rodengen.

26. Ibid.
27. David Yeager, interview.
28. Phillip Yeager, interview by Jeffrey Rodengen.

**Chapter Five Sidebar:**
**The Legacy of Joyce Yeager**

1. Phillip Yeager, written correspondence to Ann Gossy, 4 April 2006.
2. Ibid.

**Chapter Five Sidebar:**
**Dick Rogan**

1. Phillip Yeager, written correspondence to Ann Gossy, 22 December 2006.

**Chapter Five Sidebar:**
**Remembering Joyce Yeager**

1. Mark Yeager, written correspondence to Ann Gossy, April 2006.
2. Thomas Hardin, correspondence via e-mail to Ann Gossy, February 2006.
3. Phillip Yeager, written correspondence to Ann Gossy, 4 April 2006.

**Chapter Six**

1. David Zeilstra, interview by Jeffrey L. Rodengen, digital recording, 22 February 2006, Write Stuff Enterprises, Inc.
2. Dan Hardman, interview by Jeffrey L. Rodengen, digital recording, 30 September 2005, Write Stuff Enterprises, Inc.
3. Joe Wallace, interview by Jeffrey L. Rodengen, digital recording, 12 October 2005, Write Stuff Enterprises, Inc.
4. Bill Schmidt, interview by Jeffrey L. Rodengen, digital recording, 11 October 2005, Write Stuff Enterprises, Inc.
5. Jim Decker, interview by Jeffrey L. Rodengen, digital recording, 4 April, 2006, Write Stuff Enterprises, Inc.
6. Stanley Dick, interview by Jeffrey L. Rodengen, digital recording, 2 February 2006, Write Stuff Enterprises, Inc.
7. Donna Dick, interview by Jeffrey L. Rodengen, digital recording, 8 February 2006, Write Stuff Enterprises, Inc.
8. Joe Wallace, interview.
9. Mark Yeager, interview by Jeffrey L. Rodengen, digital recording, 31 August 2005, Write Stuff Enterprises, Inc.
10. Ron Hazlett, interview by Jeffrey L. Rodengen, digital recording, 3 October 2005, Write Stuff Enterprises, Inc.
11. David Zeilstra, interview.
12. Mark Yeager, interview.
13. Thomas Hardin, interview by Jeffrey L. Rodengen, digital recording, 15 February 2006, Write Stuff Enterprises, Inc.
14. David Yeager, interview by Jeffrey L. Rodengen, digital recording, 1 September 2005, Write Stuff Enterprises, Inc.
15. Phillip Yeager, written correspondence to Ann Gossy, 4 April 2006.
16. Hub Annual Report, 2000.
17. Ibid.
18. Phillip Yeager, written correspondence to Ann Gossy, 22 December, 2006.
19. "NASD Notice to Members," http://www.nasd.com/.
20. Phillip Yeager, interview by Jeffrey L. Rodengen, digital recording, 1 September 2005, Write Stuff Enterprises, Inc.
21. Thomas Hardin, interview.
22. Ibid.
23. Stephen Cosgrove interview by Jeffrey L. Rodengen, digital

recording, 31 August 2005, Write Stuff Enterprises, Inc.

24. "Hub Plans to Buy APC Segment," *Railway Age*, May 1996.

25. Thomas Hardin, interview.

26. Megan Santosus, "Working on the Railroad," *CIO*, 15 February 1996.

27. Brian Avery, interview by Jeffrey L. Rodengen, digital recording, 28 March 2006, Write Stuff Enterprises, Inc.

28. Thomas Hardin, interview.

29. Carl Nolte, Kenneth Howe, "Transcontinental Rail Gridlock," *San Francisco Chronicle*, 11 October 1997.

30. Phillip Yeager, interview by Jeffrey L. Rodengen.

31. Hub Annual Report, 1996.

32. Ron Hazlett, interview.

33. Joe Wallace, interview.

34. Hub Annual Report, 1997.

35. Bill Schmidt, interview.

36. Jim Decker, interview.

37. Phillip Yeager, written correspondence to Ann Gossy, 4 April 2006.

38. Hub Annual Report, 1997.

39. Phillip Yeager, interview by Carolyn Quayle, Oral History Interview transcript, the Intermodal Founding Fathers of North America Conference, 28 July 1999.

40. "Transcontinental Rail Gridlock."

41. Phillip Yeager, interview by Jeffrey L. Rodengen.

42. "Transcontinental Rail Gridlock."

43. Hub Annual Report, 1998.

44. Thomas Hardin, interview.

45. Phillip Yeager, interview by Jeffrey L. Rodengen.

46. Hub Annual Report, 1997.

47. Phillip Yeager, written correspondence.

48. Harry Inda, interview by Jeffrey L. Rodengen, digital recording, 11 October 2005, Write Stuff Enterprises, Inc.

49. Phillip Yeager, written correspondence.

50. "Hub Announces Restructuring," *PR Newswire*, 10 March 1998.

51. "Hub Acquires Quality Intermodal," *PR Newswire*, 10 March 1998.

52. Hub Annual Report, 1998.

53. Thomas Hardin, written correspondence to Ann Gossy, February 2006.

54. "Hub Claims UP Service 'Bottomed Out,'" *Traffic World*, 10 November 1997.

55. Rip Watson, "BNSF Taps Hub to Manage Boxes," *Journal of Commerce*, 14 April 1998.

56. Thomas Hardin, interview.

57. Steve Branscum, interview by Jeffrey L. Rodengen, digital recording, 7 April 2006, Write Stuff Enterprises, Inc.

58. Thomas Hardin, interview.

59. Ibid.

60. Rip Watson, "BNSF Taps Hub to Manage Boxes," *Journal of Commerce*, 14 April 1998.

61. Jack Burke, "Hub Tries New Container Approach," *Traffic World*, 20 April 1998.

62. Thomas Hardin, interview.

63. Phillip Yeager, interview by Carolyn Quayle.

64. Hub Annual Report, 2000.

65. Phillip Yeager, interview by Carolyn Quayle.

66. Connie Sheffield, interview by Jeffrey L. Rodengen, digital recording, 13 February

2006, Write Stuff Enterprises, Inc.
67. Ibid.
68. Thomas Malloy, interview by Jeffrey L. Rodengen, digital recording, 13 February 2006, Write Stuff Enterprises, Inc.
69. Lillian Barrone, interview by Jeffrey L. Rodengen, digital recording, 3 February 2006, Write Stuff Enterprises, Inc.
70. David Yeager, interview.
71. Chrystal Caruthers, "Lombard's Hub Group to Buy Out Minority Stake," *Chicago Daily Herald*, 24 March 1999.
72. Mark Yeager, interview.
73. David Zeilstra, interview.
74. David Yeager, interview.
75. Thomas Hardin, interview.
76. Brian Avery, interview.
77. Thomas Hardin, written correspondence to Ann Gossy, February 2006.
78. Thomas Hardin, interview.
79. Joseph Bonney, "Phillip Yeager's Hub Group," *American Shipper*, May 1991.
80. Phillip Yeager, written correspondence.
81. "Form 10-K," Hub Group, Inc., 22 March 2002.

82. Phillip Yeager, Presentation from the Intermodal Founding Fathers of North America Conference, 27–29 July 1999.
83. Phillip Yeager, personal correspondence to Intermodal Transportation Institute, 8 December 1998.
84. Presentation from the Intermodal Founding Fathers of North America Conference.
85. Hub Annual Report, 1999.

**Chapter Six Sidebar: Hub Celebrates 25 Years**

1. Thomas Hardin, interview by Jeffrey L. Rodengen, digital recording, 15 February 2006, Write Stuff Enterprises, Inc.
2. Phillip Yeager, written correspondence to Ann Gossy, 4 April 2006.
3. Thomas Hardin, interview.

**Chapter Six Sidebar: Intermodal Founding Fathers**

1. Phillip Yeager, Presentation from the Intermodal Founding Fathers of North America Conference, 27–29 July 1999.

2. Ibid.
3. Presentation from the Intermodal Founding Fathers of North America Conference.
4. Ibid.
5. Phillip Yeager, Highlight Notes for Presentation from the Intermodal Founding Fathers of North America Conference, 27–29 July 1999.

**Chapter Seven**

1. "Dot Com Boom," http://en.wikipedia.org/wiki/Dot_Com_Boom/.
2. Mark Yeager, interview by Jeffrey L. Rodengen, digital recording, 31 August 2005, Write Stuff Enterprises, Inc.
3. David Yeager, interview by Jeffrey L. Rodengen, digital recording, 1 September 2005, Write Stuff Enterprises, Inc.
4. Mark Yeager, interview.
5. Dennis Polsen, interview by Jeffrey L. Rodengen, digital recording, 31 August 2005, Write Stuff Enterprises, Inc.
6. Mark Yeager, interview.
7. Dennis Polsen, interview.
8. Ibid.

9. David Yeager, interview.

10. Kevin Knapp, "Corporate Guide to Chicago's Publicly Held Companies," *Crain's Chicago Business*, 8 June 2000.

11. Donald Maltby, Jr., interview by Jeffrey L. Rodengen, digital recording, 31 August 2005, Write Stuff Enterprises, Inc.

12. "CYSIVE, Inc., Launches Phase Two of Hub Group, Inc.'s, Online Shipment Tracking System," *Railway Age*, 1 September 2000.

13. "Hub Group, Inc., Anticipates a Shortfall in EPS," *PR Newswire*, 2 October 2000.

14. David Yeager, interview.

15. Mark Yeager, interview.

16. John Gallagher, "New Look at IMC Hub," *Traffic World*, 11 December 2000.

17. Dennis Polsen, interview.

18. "New Look at IMC Hub."

19. Jude Troppoli, interview by Jeffrey L. Rodengen, digital recording, 7 February, 2006, Write Stuff Enterprises, Inc.

20. Dennis Polsen, interview.

21. Susan Nadeau, "B2B Exchanges Come of Age," *Chicago Tribune*, 2 April 2001.

22. Hub Annual Report, 2001.

23. Phillip Yeager, interview by Jeffrey L. Rodengen, digital recording, 1 September 2005, Write Stuff Enterprises, Inc.

24. "Hub Group, Inc., Anticipates a Shortfall in EPS," *PR Newswire*, 25 September 2001.

25. Phillip Yeager, written correspondence to Ann Gossy, 4 April 2006.

26. "Hub Group, Inc., Anticipates a Shortfall in EPS."

27. Phillip Yeager, written correspondence.

28. Jim Comerford, interview by Jeffrey L. Rodengen, digital recording, 8 March 2006, Write Stuff Enterprises, Inc.

29. "SLS Renews Logistics Deal with Hub Group," *Business Wire*, 13 August 2001.

30. Thomas Hardin, interview by Jeffrey L. Rodengen, digital recording, 1 September 2005, Write Stuff Enterprises, Inc.

31. Mark Yeager, interview.

32. Hub Annual Report, 2001.

33. David Yeager, interview.

34. Phillip Yeager, written correspondence.

35. Mark Yeager, interview.

36. David Yeager, interview.

37. Christopher Kravas, interview by Jeffrey L. Rodengen, digital recording, 1 September 2005, Write Stuff Enterprises, Inc.

38. Mark Yeager, interview by Ann Gossy, digital recording, 11 May 2006, Write Stuff Enterprises, Inc.

39. Hub Annual Report, 2001.

40. Phillip Yeager, interview by Jeffrey L. Rodengen.

41. Mike Comerford, "Hub Group Finds Accounting Error," *Chicago Daily Herald*, 14 February 2002.

42. John Gallagher, "Hub Regroups," *Traffic World*, 4 March 2002.

43. Clayton Boyce, "Consider the Source," *Traffic World*, 4 March 2002.

44. John Gallagher, "Moving Ahead," *Traffic World*, 8 July 2002.

45. Hub Annual Report, 2002.

46. "Moving Ahead."

47. "Hub Group, Inc., Names Two Vice Presidents," *Business Wire*, 9 August 2002.

48. Thomas White, interview by Jeffrey L.

Rodengen, digital recording, 1 September 2005, Write Stuff Enterprises, Inc.

49. David Yeager, interview.
50. "Hub Group, Inc., Announces the Next Phase of Its Long-Term Improvement Program," *PR Newswire*, 2 October 2002.
51. "Hub Group, TMM partner on Mexico logistics," JoC Online, 29 October 2002.
52. David Yeager, interview.
53. Dan Hardman, interview by Jeffrey L. Rodengen, digital recording, 30 September 2005, Write Stuff Enterprises, Inc.
54. Hub Annual Report, 2002.
55. "Hub Group to Remain Independent," *PR Newswire*, 19 November 2002.
56. Joseph Bonney, "Phillip Yeager's Hub Group," *American Shipper*, May 1991.
57. Mark Yeager, interview.
58. Thomas White, interview by Jeffrey L. Rodengen, digital recording, 1 September 2005, Write Stuff Enterprises, Inc.
59. Mark Yeager, interview.
60. James Gaw, interview by Jeffrey L. Rodengen,

digital recording, 1 September 2005, Write Stuff Enterprises, Inc.
61. Ibid.
62. Thomas White, interview.
63. Dan Hardman, interview.
64. James Gaw, interview.
65. Thomas White, interview.
66. Phillip Yeager, interview by Jeffrey L. Rodengen.
67. Mark Yeager, interview.
68. Thomas Hardin, interview.
69. Phillip Yeager, interview by Jeffrey L. Rodengen.
70. Thomas White, interview.
71. Mark Yeager, interview.
72. James Gaw, interview.
73. Phillip Yeager, interview by Jeffrey L. Rodengen.
74. Thomas White, interview.
75. John Gallagher, "Realigning Intermodal," *Traffic World*, 15 December 2003.
76. Thomas White, interview.
77. "Realigning Intermodal."

**Chapter Eight**

1. Phillip Yeager, "Facing the Future: Observations and Predictions from 186 Industry Leaders," supplemental issue of *Journal of Commerce*, 12 January 2004.
2. Mark Yeager, "Hub Group at Deutsche Bank Securities Transportation

Conference," transcript, 16 February 2005.
3. Stephen Cosgrove, interview by Jeffrey L. Rodengen, digital recording, 31 August 2005, Write Stuff Enterprises, Inc.
4. David Marsh, interview by Jeffrey L. Rodengen, digital recording, 31 August 2005, Write Stuff Enterprises, Inc.
5. Stephen Cosgrove, interview.
6. James Gaw, interview by Jeffrey L. Rodengen, digital recording, 1 September 2005, Write Stuff Enterprises, Inc.
7. Thomas White, "Hub Group at Raymond James Annual Institutional Investors Conference," transcript, 9 March 2005.
8. John Gallagher, "Realigning Intermodal," *Traffic World*, 15 December 2003.
9. Thomas Hardin, interview by Jeffrey L. Rodengen, digital recording, 15 February 2006, Write Stuff Enterprises, Inc.
10. James Gaw, interview.
11. David Yeager, "Hub Group at Deutsche Bank Securities Transportation

Conference," transcript, 11 February 2004.

12. Brian Avery, interview by Jeffrey L. Rodengen, digital recording, 28 March 2006, Write Stuff Enterprises, Inc.

13. Lee Murphy, "Tide of Caution Lifts Shipper Hub Group," *Crain's Chicago Business*, 12 April 2004.

14. "Hub Reorganization Pays Off," *Traffic World*, 12 May 2004.

15. Thomas White, interview by Jeffrey L. Rodengen, digital recording, 1 September 2005, Write Stuff Enterprises, Inc.

16. Thomas Hardin, interview.

17. Mike McClellan, interview by Jeffrey L. Rodengen, digital recording, 8 February 2006, Write Stuff Enterprises, Inc.

18. Mark Yeager, interview by Ann Gossy, digital recording, 11 May 2006, Write Stuff Enterprises, Inc.

19. Phillip Yeager, interview by Jeffrey Rodengen, digital recording, 1 September 2005, Write Stuff Enterprises, Inc.

20. Prospectus, Hub Group, Inc., 28 June 2004.

21. Robert Mottley, "Intermodal Logistics,"

22. Phillip Yeager, interview by Jeffrey L. Rodengen.

23. "Intermodal Logistics."

24. JDM & Associates, "Target Names Hub Group 'Intermodal Carrier of the Year,'" 20 July 2004.

25. Ibid.

26. "Hub Group Wins the Home Depot's Intermodal Carrier of the Year Award," *PR Newswire*, 3 November 2004.

27. Bob Tita, "Cost Cuts Drive Hub's Profit Surge," *Crain's Chicago Business*, 4 October 2004.

28. "HUBG: Enters Option Agreement for Sale of Subsidiary for $11.3M," *Comtex News Network*, 16 November 2004.

29. Mark Yeager, interview by Ann Gossy.

30. "13 Transportation Companies on *Forbes* List," *The Trucker*, 10 January 2005.

31. "Hub Group Cruises Higher on Bear Stearns Upgrade," *CBS MarketWatch*, 16 December 2004.

32. "HUBG: Yeager Appointed as President; Replaces Hardin," *Comtex News Network*, 6 January 2005.

*American Shipper*, September 2004.

33. "Yeager to Head Hub Group," *Traffic World*, 24 March 2005.

34. Thomas Hardin, interview.

35. Mark Yeager, interview by Ann Gossy.

36. "Hub Sets Quarter Profit Record," *Chicago Daily Herald*, 9 February 2005.

37. "*Fortune*'s Most Admired Companies," *Fortune*, March 2004.

38. Mark Yeager, "Hub Group at Deutsche Bank Securities Transportation Conference" transcript, 16 February 2005.

39. Ibid.

40. "HUBG: Enters Equipment Purchase Contract with Shanghai Jindo," *Comtex News Network*, 8 March 2005.

41. Bill Mongelluzzo, "IMCs Becomes Asset Owners," *Journal of Commerce*, 29 August 2005.

42. Mark Yeager, interview by Jeffrey L. Rodengen, digital recording, 31 August 2005, Write Stuff Enterprises, Inc.

43. Thomas Hardin, interview.

44. David Yeager, "Hub Group at Raymond James Annual Institutional Investors Conference," transcript, 9 March 2005.

45. "Hub Group Announces New Name, Brand for Logistics Unit," *PR Newswire*, 21 March 2005.
46. Ibid.
47. "*Fortune*'s Most Admired Companies," *Fortune*, March, 2005.
48. "Hub Group: Record 1Q Earnings," *Traffic World*, 21 April 2005.
49. "Lighting Hub's Tunnel," *Traffic World*, 22 June 2005.
50. "Hub Group, Inc., Reports Record Earnings for the Second Quarter," *PR Newswire*, 20 July 2005.
51. "Hub Group Profit Sets Quarterly Record," *Chicago Daily Herald*, 22 October 2005.
52. Ted Pincus, "Hub Group's Growth Fast as a Speeding Train," *Chicago Sun-Times*, 4 October 2005.
53. Ibid.
54. Phillip Yeager, "Facing the Future: Observations and Predictions," supplemental issue of *Journal of Commerce*, 9 January 2006.
55. John Gallagher, "Largest IMC Acquires Comtrak to Build More

Business," *Traffic World*, 30 January 2006.
56. David Zeilstra, interview by Jeffrey L. Rodengen, digital recording, 22 February 2006, Write Stuff Enterprises, Inc.
57. Mike Bruns, interview by Jeffrey L. Rodengen, digital recording, 10 March 2006, Write Stuff Enterprises, Inc.
58. "Largest IMC Acquires Comtrak to Build More Business."
59. David Beasley, interview by Jeffrey L. Rodengen, digital recording, 7 February 2006, Write Stuff Enterprises, Inc.
60. Steve Rand, interview by Jeffrey L. Rodengen, digital recording, 2 February 2006, Write Stuff Enterprises, Inc.
61. George Baima, interview by Jeffrey L. Rodengen, digital recording, 7 March 2006, Write Stuff Enterprises, Inc.
62. Jim Ronchetto, interview by Jeffrey L. Rodengen, digital recording, 3 February 2006, Write Stuff Enterprises, Inc.
63. John Gallagher, "Hub Group on a Roll," *Traffic World*, 20 February 2006.
64. Ibid.

65. "Hub Completes Comtrak Acquisition," *Traffic World*, 1 March 2006.
66. Joe Egertson, interview by Jeffrey L. Rodengen, digital recording, 28 December 2005, Write Stuff Enterprises, Inc.
67. Mike Carrol, interview by Jeffrey L. Rodengen, digital recording, 7 March 2006, Write Stuff Enterprises, Inc.
68. "Index to the Fortune 500 and the Fortune 1,000," *Fortune*, 3 April 2006.
69. "Hub Group, Inc., Reports Record First Quarter 2006 Earnings," *PR Newswire*, 12 April 2006.
70. Phillip Yeager, interview by Ann Gossy, digital recording, 12 May 2006, Write Stuff Enterprises, Inc.
71. Stephen Cosgrove, interview by Jeffrey L. Rodengen, digital recording, 31 August 2005, Write Stuff Enterprises, Inc.
72. Mark Yeager, interview.
73. Phillip Yeager, interview by Carolyn Quayle, Oral History Interview transcript, The Intermodal Founding Fathers of North

America Conference, 28 July 1999.

**Chapter Eight Sidebar:
Hub's Strategic Plan**

1. David Yeager, interview by Jeffrey L. Rodengen, digital recording, 21 July 2006, Write Stuff Enterprises, Inc.

**Chapter Eight Sidebar:
More Than Intermodal**

1. Mark Yeager, interview by Ann Gossy, digital recording, 14 August 2006, Write Stuff Enterprises, Inc.

**Chapter Eight Sidebar:
Hub's Big Red Boxes**

1. Brian Avery, interview by Jeffrey L. Rodengen, digital recording, 28 March 2006, Write Stuff Enterprises, Inc.
2. James Gaw, interview by Jeffrey L. Rodengen, digital recording, 1 September 2005, Write Stuff Enterprises, Inc.

3. Brian Avery, interview.
4. Mark Yeager, interview by Jeffrey L. Rodengen, digital recording, 31 August 2005, Write Stuff Enterprises, Inc.

**Chapter Eight Sidebar:
Hub: Past, Present, and Future**

1. Phillip Yeager, interview by Jeffrey L. Rodengen, digital recording, 21 July 2006, Write Stuff Enterprises, Inc.

# INDEX

*Page numbers in italics indicate photographs.*